GEORGE ELIOT
& the Novel of Vocation

GEORGE ELIOT
& the Novel of Vocation

Alan Mintz

Harvard University Press
Cambridge, Massachusetts
London, England
1978

Publication of this volume has been aided by a grant
from the Andrew W. Mellon Foundation

Library of Congress Cataloging in Publication Data
Mintz, Alan L.
  George Eliot and the novel of vocation.
  Includes index.
  1. Eliot, George, pseud., i.e. Marian Evans,
afterwards Cross, 1819-1880. Middlemarch.
2. Vocation in literature. I. Title.
PR4662.M5   823'.8   77-15510
ISBN 0-674-34873-7

FOR MY PARENTS

PREFACE

The twentieth century has seen many changes in the valuation of work. For Americans who came of age during the Great Depression the issue of work was most often a question of whether one was lucky enough to have any, not what kind of work was worth doing. When there is heroism in sheer economic survival, work is valued as livelihood. Benefiting from the industry of their parents and from the rapidly expanding economy of the postwar years, the generation that grew up during the fifties and sixties could take the availability of work for granted. For some the new security encouraged careers of various sorts of idealism, but for many it signaled the weakening of the "work ethic" and the eclipse of work by leisure. Social analysts predicted that Americans would increasingly derive meaning not from work but from the style and quality of life outside of work, that is, not from production but from consumption. The "free time" liberated from the drudgery of work would provide an opportunity for the higher cultivation of the self, as well as horizonless new markets for consumer products and services.

The changed economic circumstances of the seventies have returned our attention to the question of work. There is not as much of it as there used to be, and the kind that has been considered by the sons and daughters of the middle class to be "attractive" work has become especially scarce. Indeed, one of the unmistakable changes in campus life in recent years has been the rush of young people to gain admission to professional schools. The particular mix of conditions that makes the professions attractive is revealing: the prestige of being neither a laborer nor a merchant nor an entrepreneur gives the professional an edge in questions of status; a privileged respectability comes from association with a "professional ethic"; a sense of power is derived from having one's services needed by others; a relative degree of financial security, though declining, still offers some insulation from the fluctuations of the labor market; there is a promise of a degree of autonomy and of control over the conditions of employment; and finally, for some, a profession is an arena for the expression of ideals of social usefulness and contribution.

The determination of women to enter the world of work has dramatized in a fresh way longstanding questions about the relationship between work and life. Women have always had work, and one of the achievements of the women's movement is the recognition of homemaking and childrearing as forms of legitimate work. But the decision of many women to leave or de-emphasize these tasks is an indication that work is being sought out as a necessary experience that has a value beyond its economic utility. Especially for women who are seeking to enter the professions and other forms of ambitious work the question whether work can serve as a positive means of self-definition and self-realization has been asked with new urgency.

There are few of us who have not at some time been concerned, often in personal terms, with questions about the nature of meaningful work, the desirable balance be-

tween work and other dimensions of life, the costs and bene-
fits of ambitious as opposed to nonambitious work. This
book deals with a moment in the nineteenth century when
there occurred a great change in attitudes toward work, a
change in which the roots of our present dilemmas are entangled. Besides properly literary questions concerning the
history of the novel, the development of George Eliot's art,
and the interplay between social institutions and the literary
imagination, this study hopes to offer some clarification of
those central issues of work and life that have not ceased to
perplex us today.

It is a pleasure to be able to acknowledge my gratitude
to my former teachers Steven Marcus and Edward Said for
the kind of direction and criticism I believe I could have received nowhere else. I also wish to thank Alan Silver, who
was a help to me at a difficult point in the writing. To
Quentin Anderson and Wayne Proudfoot and to my friends
Gail Twersky Reimer and Arnold Eisen I owe thanks for suggestions incorporated in the work. Ian Watt read several
versions of the manuscript and made invaluable suggestions.
Catherine D. Martin brought patient wisdom to the job of
copyediting. I am grateful to Isadore Twersky for his pa-
tience while this work took me away from newly assumed
tasks and to The Lady Davis Fellowship Trust of Jerusalem
for making a summer of revisions possible. The staffs of the
libraries of Tufts College and The Hebrew University of
Jerusalem were always gracious in giving assistance.

CONTENTS

GEORGE ELIOT
& the Novel
of Vocation

LADY BRACKNELL. Do you smoke?

JACK. Well, yes, I must admit I smoke.

LADY BRACKNELL. I am glad to hear it. A man should always have an occupation of some kind.

The Importance of
Being Earnest

1

IDEAS AND INSTITUTIONS

"Except for God," writes Walter Houghton, "the most popular word in the Victorian vocabulary must have been 'work.' "[1] Carlyle's denunciations of the aristocracy's idleness and his cries of "Work! Work! Work!" reverberate throughout the nineteenth century. It is understandable that a commercial society undergoing an industrial transformation would enshrine the values and activities that expedited this process. But work was praised with equal fervor by the prophets of industrialization as by its critics.[2] The enthusiasm for work is a virtual touchstone of Victorian sensibility. As reason had been to the Enlightenment, work was to the Victorians: an overarching term that sanctioned a multitude of diverse, often antagonistic positions. For some, working was the chief way of doing God's will in the world; and for others, work became a "gospel" in its own right, replacing Christianity's claims on man. For some, work was a selfless submission to one's duty that helped to further the progress of mankind; and for others work meant the development of one's natural talents and the assertion of individual genius. Finally, work was at times a therapy for the Victorian disease of introspective despair; yet the uncertainty of what, if anything, was worth doing brought its own anxiety and affliction.

Although there were exceptions, the mainstream of narrative prose fiction in the Victorian age undertook the critical representation of work with as much vigor as it did other emerging features of the industrializing society. Shocked by the realities of the new world of work, some novelists contrasted idealized images of the traditional rural craftsman and the benevolent squire with a grim depiction of the deforming conditions of factory work. Other novelists, enthralled by the spectacle of newly released energy, took pleasure in tracing the careers of highly ambitious individuals as they moved through the labyrinth of possibilities created by a society in ferment. The late novels of George Eliot are preoccupied with the question of work, especially in its relation to the middle classes. What distinguishes hers from other Victorian fiction is her refusal either to delight in or to deplore the changed nature of work in the nineteenth century. She determines instead to assess its human possibilities. In a series of complex fictional characters George Eliot examines both how far the conditions of the age made it possible for the impulse toward self-aggrandizing ambition and the impulse toward selfless contribution to society to be united in a single life, and, in addition, how that union is supported by secularized versions of older Protestant ideas about a man's calling in the world.

The claims I wish to make on behalf of George Eliot's achievement in her late works, particularly in *Middlemarch,* are far-reaching. But before the uniqueness of that achievement can be identified, it is first necessary to lay out in a systematic way some of the social forces and ideas that informed nineteenth-century attitudes toward work.

Eight closely related sociohistorical themes are at play. The first three are general: (1) the Protestant notion of calling or vocation, which is religious but not restricted to a calling to the ministry; (2) the notion of calling to the ministry, which is not necessarily Protestant; (3) the economic ideology Weber called the Protestant ethic. The remaining five are largely peculiar to the nineteenth century: (4) the extreme social mobility made possible by the rapidly expanding economy; (5) the general results of the division of labor, leading to a wider degree of choice in employment; (6) the consequence of this specialization of function in middle-class career professionalism, especially as it is linked to the availability of new sources of technical knowledge and to the establishment of professional associations; (7) the consequences of this in the crucial and problematic nature of job-choice for the individual in a society growing more secularized, functionally differentiated, and individualistic; and (8) the secularized and Puritan version of profession expressed in a transformed idea of vocation.

Much of the literature that was alive to the social transformations of the midnineteenth century took up one or more of these themes. The idea of vocation was brought squarely into contemporary discussion by Carlyle's lectures on hero-worship, which urged the Calvinist notion that a saint is a man who is called by an outside agency to undertake some great worldly achievement; at the same time Carlyle railed against the narrowing of the scope of that achievement brought about by the division of labor. In contrast, Cardinal Newman sought in his autobiographical writings to restore to the idea of calling the older requirement that its fulfillment come through religious profession and through a life within the ministry devoted to developing and refining religious doctrines. Many other Victorians contributed other varied possibilities. John Stuart Mill's dedicated preoccupation with his intellectual development was a kind of devotion to a secular ministry. How the breakdown of doctrinal belief deprived the individual of the traditional pastoral role of the ministry was the concern of W. Hale

White in the Mark Rutherford novels. George Eliot's *The Mill on the Floss* scrutinized how the severe economic ethic, which Weber argued arose with the Protestant notion of calling, displaced sentiment and imagination.

One of the grand themes of the Victorian novel is the "careers" of ambitious young men and women — usually the orphaned and disinherited — as they rise through the tiers of a newly accessible but still highly stratified society. Because women had no direct access to the world of offices and affairs, female characters sometimes provide sharp paradigms of social ambition, as is the case with Becky Sharp in *Vanity Fair*. While a Disraeli hero might strive for a position of influence over the affairs of his country, a newcomer like Pip in *Great Expectations* may simply seek the social role of a gentleman.

More often than not, interest in the conception of a gentleman as a man who could afford not to work is eclipsed by men who exercise their ambition through an active vocation. The general division of labor changed the traditional professions and gave professional status to many new ones. Trollope's Phineas Finn novels examine the vicissitudes of career politics in the era of Reform as they condition the public life of the son of an Irish doctor. Turning to the provinces and to a different profession, Trollope's Barchester novels investigate the politics of the church at a time when the spirit of the age is at variance with the exercise of traditional ecclesiastical prerogatives. Dickens' novels encompass almost the entire world of work, from commerce and the established professions to school teaching, architecture, and engineering, and even to the new profession of private investigation. Dickens is less interested in individual careers than in how such professions as law and the civil service function as social institutions. Large portraits like those of Bounderby and Dombey, in which Dickens probes the perversion of feeling at the center of the personal lives of industrialists, stand out against a vast collection of miniatures, in which personal identity and work identity are fused into the single grotesque or comic gesture of a Fagin or a Mr. Micawber.

The increasingly anxiety-ridden dilemmas facing young men and women on the threshold of choosing a determined course of work are also much in evidence in Victorian novels. Like many a younger son, Edmund in *Mansfield Park* takes orders, but he is temporarily lured away from pursuing his career as a minister by the worldly ethos of visiting Londoners. Tantalized by the prospect of an inheritance that would release him from the necessity of work, Richard Carstone in *Bleak House* goes through the motions of trying out each of the professions; but in the end he fatally abandons himself to the lure of his expectations. The fate of women alone in the world and the meager choices available to them are the subjects of Charlotte Brontë's explorations into the world of governesses and teachers.

In contrast to the dispersion of the separate themes of work throughout Victorian literature, *Middlemarch* stands as a kind of *summa,* collecting and juxtaposing them. The unholy union of a privileged sense of calling with a dishonest business ethic is depicted in the sanctimonious machinations of the evangelical banker Bulstrode. Although the figures of Farebrother and Casaubon make it clear that the ministry is no longer a divine office, it remains an office either to be humanized, as it is by Farebrother, or to be shunned, as it is by such young men as Fred Vincy, who would enter the ministry merely for lack of property or something better to do. The portrayal of Tertius Lydgate, Middlemarch's new doctor, is a thorough examination of the problems facing a hopeful young practitioner whose profession is being reorganized and outfitted with new technical knowledge. Two of the novel's subplots are given to the problems of job choice. Fred Vincy, the idle son of a local manufacturer, would prefer to be a sporting man of independent means; yet he must find a way to mediate between his father's insistence that he enter the ministry and his sweetheart's declaration that she will never accept him if he does. There is the instructive parallel of Will Ladislaw, who realizes, after he is cut off by his cousin, that unless he is otherwise saved he will either have to put his intellectual talents out for hire or eke out a shabby life as a barrister. *Middlemarch* is principally concerned with the problems of middle-class work, but the novel also touches on other ranges of the vocational spectrum, from the dissatisfactions of the agricultural proletariat to the philanthropic aspirations of the squirearchy.

Beyond the comprehensive treatment of these themes, *Middlemarch* also represents a major aspect of work that is by and large not taken up in other novels: the experience of vocation. George Eliot saw in the rise of the professions a vehicle for a much larger idea: beyond providing a useful service or a livelihood, professional work might be in itself a significant means of self-realization and of contributing to the progress of humankind. This spiritualization of work is a secularized version of the Puritan beliefs that a man is called by God to a specific worldly vocation and that his success in it is a token of salvation. The world of *Middlemarch* partakes of a similar mixture of spirituality and worldliness, high service and self-concern. In carrying out their work, the characters of the novel are motivated both by a sense of responsibility to a higher impersonal goal and by a drive for personal redemption; they undertake (or fail to undertake) a total commitment to work methodically toward various ambitious purposes. The novel records the formation of this commitment, the roots of its motivation, and the course of its success or failure withstanding the threats posed by the solicitations of society and the contradictions of the self.

Tertius Lydgate, who is eager to make a name for himself and also to contribute to the nascent science of physiology and to reform his profession, is the outstanding exemplar of the contradictions of vocation. But Lydgate is not the only one affected. The ideal of vocation suffuses the whole range of work-related themes in *Middlemarch* with a kind of desperate spirituality. One senses, for example, that if Will Ladislaw or Fred Vincy should make the wrong choice of profession, the consequences would entail much more than mere unhappiness or poverty. The sadness of a Farebrother who missed his vocation, the damnation of a Bulstrode who perverted his calling, the spiritual death of a Casaubon who failed at his — all these human fates come into special perspective by virtue of their relation to a single spiritual value. Ultimately, vocation is viewed as a desire that by definition cannot be fulfilled. Dorothea Brooke does not desist from seeking the satisfactions of high achievement in the world, even though as a woman entry into a formal vocation is barred to her. The displacements of vocational desire constitute one of the central subjects of *Middlemarch*.

The special greatness of *Middlemarch* lies not only in its probing of the contradictions of vocation but also in its construction of such commanding figures as Lydgate and Dorothea, who comprehend those contradictions. Writing without a similar ideological underpinning, Dickens dealt extensively with questions of self-aggrandizement and self-lessness, ranging, to be sure, far more freely over the scale of social class and the varieties of social institutions and political questions. With a small number of exceptions, however, Dickens avoided the full study of any single, total consciousness; he chose instead to distribute the contradictions of vocation among the dozens of characters that populate each novel. Therefore, to find more complete analogues to George Eliot's deeper concern with vocation, and thus put *Middlemarch* in its proper larger context, we must look to the great biographies and autobiographies of such men as Carlyle, Mill, and Newman.

The more immediate task is to trace the nonliterary sources for George Eliot's use of vocation as the thematic structure of *Middlemarch*. I shall seek to reconstruct the way in which George Eliot appropriated a secularized version of the Puritan notion of calling in order to transfigure a new form of middle-class work and produced a new way of representing character in fiction.

"Calling" and "vocation," as terms to describe worldly rather than clerical pursuits, are products of the Reformation.[3] Luther originated the new usage of the term in translating as *Beruf* the key words from the Apocryphal book the Wisdom of Ben Sirach (9:20, 21): "Persevere in your duty, take pleasure in doing it, and grow old in your work." Although at the outset of his theological career Luther regarded worldly activity as morally neutral, as medieval scholastics had regarded eating and drinking, the idea of the calling grew in importance while his opposition to the monastic life intensified. Luther's emphasis on the particular worldly station to which an individual was called was based on the Pauline strain in the New Testament and the belief that, since the redemption was imminent, a man might well persevere in the worldly occupation in which the call of the Lord had found him. This conception of calling, in its insistence that the existing structure of society is a direct manifestation of divine will, was highly traditional. But the very idea that occupation and livelihood could be identified as a direct and positive means of salvation was Luther's innovation. With Luther's teaching, the relationship between the active and the contemplative life was reversed: the fulfillment of duty in worldly affairs was now valued as "the highest form which the moral activity of the individual could assume."[4]

Weber's *The Protestant Ethic and the Spirit of Capitalism* (1904-05), in addition to its conceptual brilliance, is particularly valuable for the study of English literature. Almost all its sources are English Puritan documents and thus are useful to our purpose, whatever may be thought of the truth of Weber's theories as regards other countries. Weber's particular interpretation of Puritanism is useful in another way as well. The normative conception of Puritanism Weber presented was largely based on documents selected from the movement's later, seventeenth-century phase. This phase, especially as it is given literary treatment in Bunyan's *The Pilgrim's Progress*, is — conveniently for our purposes — the strain of Puritanism which had the most influence on George Eliot. Moreover, since George Eliot employed the idea of calling in its worldly but nonmaterial sense, it will not be necessary to adjudicate the controversy over Weber's view that Protestantism led to modern capitalism. Our aim will be to understand the implications of the doctrine of the calling for the organization of human character in general.

The words "vocation" and "calling"[5] first appear in English in the Bible translations of the Reformers in the first half of the sixteenth century, primarily in reference to I Corinthians 7:20: "Let every man abide in the same calling to which he was called" (Cranmer, 1539, and King James, 1611), and "abide in the state wherein he was called" (Tindale, 1534, and Geneva, 1557), where "calling" is used to translate the Greek *klēsis* and the Latin *vocation*. The static notion of calling as a station or location in the divinely ordained order of society soon changed. The word came to designate in plain speech the *means* whereby a man earns a livelihood, his occupation or business, while retaining the implication that one's occupation has the force of divine sanction behind it. The usage was so well established by the end of the sixteenth century (at least among the Reformers) that Shakespeare could successfully mock the indiscriminate reach of its implied sanctions:

Prince. I see a good amendment of life in thee — from praying to purse-taking.

Falstaff. Why, Hal, 'tis my vocation, Hal. 'Tis no sin for a man to labor in his vocation.

(*Henry IV* Part I, I.ii.96-99)

Finally, William Perkins' *A Treatise of the Vocations, or Callings of Men* (1603) did a great deal to raise the idea of calling to the level of doctrine, as did the great synods of the seventeenth century, especially in the Westminster Confession of 1647, the tenth chapter of which is entitled "Of Effectual Calling."

As a doctrine rather than as a part of plain speech, calling is a corollary of the central Calvinist teaching of predestination. Some men are "predestined unto everlasting life" and others to everlasting death, and in view of man's fall into the state of sin, there is absolutely no way for him "by his own strength to convert himself, or to prepare himself" for his own salvation.[6] From man's natural state of sin and death it is only God, at His appointed time, who can "effectually call" man. The doctrinal impossibility of achieving one's own salvation, together with the practical impossibility of knowing definitely who has been saved, became a source of immense anxiety to the Puritan saint. It is precisely here, in the anxiety of predestination and the strategies for its mitigation, that Weber saw the groundwork of an ethic which conduced to certain forms of economic activity. To ease the fears of their congregations Puritan preachers exhorted them to consider themselves as if they were already chosen and to combat as work of the devil any temptation to doubt their possession of grace. Thus, even though salvation itself could not be forced, one could achieve a *certitudo salutis,* an inner conviction of the certainty of one's salvation, a sense of self-confidence about one's unknown and unknowable election. This much, at least, could be achieved through works. Although works could not in themselves affect the essential state of one's soul, they could at the very minimum serve as intelligible signs of one's arrival, as tokens of election produced by one's own diligence and application.

The anxiety of predestination could be allayed by working hard in one's calling and thereby producing the visible indications of success. A God-fearing man devoted himself to his calling with a methodical application that left no moment of his life, except those necessary for family and chapel, unavailable to the interests of his calling. This systematic mobilization of energies was accomplished by the suppression of many forms of spontaneous, secular enjoyment of the body, of art, of nature, of anything that might lead away from the task at hand and open up an idle space in which the devil could establish a foothold. The goal was to keep in motion, to keep working, to exploit each moment systematically. That this state of perpetual activity left little time for the enjoyment of what was materially gained by it was an essential point for Weber: when production far outstrips consumption, and profits are reinvested rather than expended, that is to say, when a commitment to continuous labor in the world is coupled with an aescetic refusal to enjoy the world, then there exist conditions of "rationality" sufficient for modern capitalism to emerge. Unlike Luther's traditionalism, which urged men to remain in the station to which God had been pleased to call them, the new doctrine urged men tirelessly to improve their lot; they need not fear the corruption of success because it was ultimately not for themselves that they worked.

This ethic had the undisputed incidental advantage of offering a positive valuation of individual action in the world. Man's secular activity need no longer unfold in a contaminated space that inherently compromised his chances for salvation. Now that the spiritual hegemony of the contemplative life had been overturned, the world was the only place left for man, and it was on the basis of his success there that he would now be judged. The fact that intense activity, however disciplined and methodical, could now work in favor of man's spiritual well-being could be counted as itself a liberation of sorts, as could the fact that men now had within their own means the power to affirm their selfhood.

If the doctrine of the calling made successful inroads against the anxiety of predestination, it also occasioned anxieties of its own. According to Calvinist theology, although all the elect received a "general" calling to salvation, it was only through a "particular" or "certain" calling, that is through a particular identifiable and established occupation, that this end could be secured. Determining what precisely that calling was involved identifying which among a man's inner urges was a providential prompting and which was the work of the devil. What we today call occupational choice was no mere matter of discovering what one did well and was happiest doing, but rather a solemn deliberation whose consequences were ultimate.[7] Working in the wrong calling or working irresponsibly or hypocritically was, similarly, not merely a personal failure but a failure to live up to the demands of a larger ideal of stewardship. The Puritan saint worked the world as a trust, and if he failed to "maximize his production," it was not only his own estate he was impoverishing but God's glory. Against the accumulating pressures of uncertainty and self-doubt, moreover, there was no sanctioned periodic release corresponding to the remission offered by the confessional. This was exactly the point: there should be no discontinuity or interruption in the systematic amassing of the worldly indications of salvation. In the words of one Puritan minister, what was demanded was "continuous labor in a calling and not occasional good deeds."[8]

Not the least among the causes of anxiety for the saint was his deep spiritual isolation. He stood directly before an absolute, transcendental God without the mediation of a church to offer the security of hierarchy, sacraments, tradition, and an authoritative interpretation of God's wishes. He and he alone was responsible for his own salvation, and the discharge of this responsibility required the constant examination and reexamination of his inner moral life, a bookkeeping procedure not unlike his mercantile transactions. Because he trusted exclusively in God, he was wary and distrustful of friendship and other personal ties that might draw him away from obedience to divine providence. Not only friendship but neighborhood, guild, and town were also suspect, because they did not contribute directly to, and in fact deflected him from, this one goal. Chief among these dangers was the family, whose claims based on blood and sentiment could easily conflict with the saint's single-minded pursuit of salvation.[9] The reader of *The Pilgrim's Progress,* a document of late Puritanism, cannot easily forget the book's opening scene in which Christian, convulsed by the realization that he is condemned to die, determines at all costs to escape from the city of Destruction. "Now he had not run far from his own door, but his Wife and children perceiving it, began to cry after him to return; but the Man put his fingers to his Ears, and ran on crying, Life, Life, Eternal Life; so he looked not behind him, but fled toward the middle of the Plain."[10] Christian is in flight from a particular kind of family configuration: the patriarchal family and its function as an enforcer of received values. The family could be converted into an instrument of God rather than an impediment to His will if the conjugal relation was viewed as a partnership between two individuals for the joint pursuit of salvation. During the rise of Puritanism alliances tended not to be arranged on the basis of inherited property but to be elected out of mutual love and with an eye toward spiritual compatibility.[11] Since the uncertain certainty of salvation was gained by worldly activity, the saint sought in a wife a women who could serve, if not always as a spiritual partner, then at least as a helpmate in affairs of business. Thus in marriage, as in all aspects of his activity, the saint sought to increase the instrumental rationality of his life vis-à-vis its ultimate ends.

At this point we shall turn again to nineteenth-century social history and the particular consequences for the middle classes of the general division of labor. In George Eliot's world the older theological ideal colored a new set of social institutions. Although they were most dramatically evident in the factory system, the effects of the division of labor were not limited to one class or even to economic relations alone. Political, administrative, and judicial functions, as well as aesthetic and scientific ones, became increasingly specialized and created new and separate bodies of techniques and new occupational applications of them. The world of *Middlemarch* is poised at this threshold of giving way to the pressures of specialization. Two characters, Caleb Garth and Mr. Brooke, hold on to the ideal of many-sidedness; but neither belongs to the present: one is bathed in George Eliot's nostalgia and the other is pelted with ridicule. Middlemarch society is clearly moving toward the separate sovereignties of scientific farming, finance, manufacture, scholarship, novel-writing, the several occupations of politics, scientific discovery, and clinical medicine. (One source of the tragedy of Lydgate, the main representative of professional life, is that he mistakenly imagines that he can combine the pursuit of the last two.)

The realignment of social forces precipitated by the specialization of function is most evident in the rise and establishment of the professions. Although for centuries there had always been the "ancient three plus two"—the clergy, law, and medicine, in addition to the army and the navy—the nineteenth century saw the rise and establishment of the professional status of many other specialized groups, such as accountants, engineers, surveyors, school teachers, journalists, and, under a different set of circumstances, politicians.[12] In most cases the process whereby an occupational group was "professionalized" followed similar lines.

Professionalization, to begin with, depended upon the existence of a body of specialized techniques whose mastery required apprenticeship or schooling. This expertise was offered to the public as a service in exchange for an established fee, the fee being paid not for a merchandise commodity but for the benefit of an intellectual or technical consultation. Essential to the consolidation of a profession

14

was the emergence of a single professional organization that represented the group in the larger society and regulated it from within. The functions of the professional organization were to fix minimum qualifications for practice, to censure unethical behavior, usually by establishing some kind of professional ethical code, and, especially in the case of groups whose professional status was not yet fully acknowledged, to create a monopoly on licensing, thus restricting the numbers and increasing the prestige of accredited members.[13]

The professions became extraordinarily significant in the nineteenth century, because they enabled technical rationality to be combined with rising social status. Professional status worked in two directions: it enabled the younger sons of the upper classes to work for a living without sacrificing their positions as gentlemen, and it enabled ambitious young men from the lower middle classes to achieve the status of gentlemen by dint of their professional energies. Thus for the former, professional work was a way of cleansing the stigma attached to living from money neither inherited nor accruing from land, and for the latter, it was a means of accumulating, through one's talent and energy, enough capital to provide one's sons with inherited income and even land.

The professions, moreover, provided a means of combining the exigencies of livelihood with the pursuit of individual idealism. Just prior to full professionalization, a profession was typically populated by numbers of freely operating individuals: charlatans and quacks, as well as innovators and reformers who, on the strength of their energetic contributions, came to be called the founders of the profession. Tertius Lydgate, the physician-hero of *Middlemarch,* hopes through his projected discoveries and reforms to achieve this stature; his career is set in the individualist phase of the modern medical profession, just before the establishment of the British Medical Association.

The status, income, and legitimacy brought by the establishment of a profession did not eliminate the costs of specialization, which were paid in different ways by all whose lives were transformed by the division of labor. The skilled professional, especially if he operated in a provincial setting, often had to practice his profession in isolation from others who shared his knowledge and interests and also from fellow townsfolk who might be suspicious of his ingenuity and cosmopolitanism. Mistrust was frequently the response of older professional colleagues, who resented the introduction of new techniques and other signs of rationalization. The independence of the young professional was further qualified by his need for substantial financial backing from his family during the initial years of practice, when he could not support himself. Moreover, in the closing years of the century, the rapidly expanding bodies of information in law, medicine, and engineering, for which no training could provide adequately, put the professional in constant danger of demoralization and obsolescence. Finally, the more successful the man, the more work claimed his life and in the process weakened his ties to such traditional institutions as family and church. Driven by his ambitions or sought after for his services, he became less available to the range of affective experiences beyond work.

Many social thinkers saw in specialization and the general division of labor the basis for great hope. Herbert Spencer — and Emile Durkheim after him — saw in the advance of society from the simple to the complex a sign of evolutionary progress. Comparing societies to living organisms, Spencer argued that the coherence threatened by heterogeneity would be guaranteed by the integrating effects of human language and emotions. Karl Marx's is one of the few voices in the century to question directly the value of the division of labor. According to Marx, the division of labor has deleterious effects on man's nature, shaping him in limited and specific ways that mirror the specialization of work tasks and driving an unnatural wedge between "intellectual and material activity, enjoyment and labor, production and consumption."[14] Marx envisioned, in the unrealized unalienated form of the division of labor, a positive paradigm for the independent fellowship of humanity. If one looked at the present division of work tasks dialectically, Marx argued, one could distinguish in the interdependence it necessitated the future outlines of "the co-operative form of the labour-process"[15] to be realized in socialist societies. In its present alienated state, however, the division of labor deforms man by forcing him unnaturally to perform one limited and repetitive operation which then becomes his entire identity as a human being. In making this analysis, Marx was one of the few thinkers who directly attacked the assumptions underlying the idea of vocation in its industrial manifestation, that is, the idea that there is one kind of work which is right for a particular individual and that it is proper, even desirable, for him to become identified with his achievement in that work.

No reader of *Middlemarch* could deny that, especially in the treatment of Lydgate, Casaubon, and Will Ladislaw, one of the novel's principal preoccupations is the relentless depiction of the social costs of specialization. Yet, strongly as George Eliot is repelled by the costs of professionalization, she is equally attracted to the possibilities, and not, surely, for the acquisition of status and income, but for the practical efficacy of knowledge in serving man. Specialization may bring isolation and trial, but without it there can be no great and useful achievement. What attracted George Eliot was the thought that at a certain moment in history — on the eve of reform — there existed the possibility that vast reservoirs of ambitious energy and practical knowledge could be released on behalf of the great causes of the age: scientific discovery, philanthropy and benevolence, political reform and humanistic learning. If a man could undertake the methodical yet ambitious pursuit of one of these high goals, then the emerging specialized forms of work did indeed hold out promise.

This would be so, that is, if a man made his profession

into a vocation. Thus seventeenth-century Puritan doctrine and emerging contemporary social institutions finally merge. In George Eliot's world the new forms of work were suffused with possibility by virtue of their association with a secularized notion of calling or vocation. The lineaments of this secularization are clear: instead of God doing the calling, it is society or duty which beckons; the call is itself experienced as a sense of inner conviction rather than as a spiritual prompting; instead of religious fervor it is "intellectual passion" which accompanies the work; the work itself is active, not contemplative, and requires methodical application; if in the classical vocational ethos a man is ambitious both for his own salvation and for the glory of God, in the new scheme he is ambitious both for his own self-realization and for the betterment of society.

Middlemarch does contain one character whose sense of vocation has undergone no secularization. Bulstrode the banker embodies an almost classical unity of religious conviction and economic practice. Bulstrode is a man whose zeal for religion is matched by his zeal for business, whose every hour is regulated by a watchful eye to his personal salvation, whose worldly actions are prescribed by the perceived dictates of a providential plan—in every outward sign, in other words, a Puritan saint. Yet his essence is pretense, hypocrisy, and deceit. Bulstrode is an example of the classical type of the hypocrite, the "smooth civil man" Puritans knew was often outwardly indistinguishable from the genuine saint. The very fact that George Eliot made this stereotype of the "unreconstructed" Calvinist entrepreneur the most thoroughly corrupt character in the novel indicates that although she carried over the Puritan doctrine of calling, it was not in the form Weber claimed it eventually took. George Eliot is interested in applying the idea of vocation to pursuits which are *in the world* but not altogether *worldly*— that is, pursuits that take place in the context of human affairs but that do not make profit their chief aim. Thus the practitioners of medicine, philanthropy, politics (of some sorts), and novel-making qualify for this designation, while, howevermuch the story is different in their own eyes, Vincy, the silk manufacturer, and Bulstrode, the banker, do not. If Weber's ideal type of the capitalist is a representation of the outcome of Puritan religion, then George Eliot is concerned more with the inspiring *idea* of vocation than with its historical consequences. Therefore, in a sense, her treatment constitutes a kind of purification or even spiritualization of the classic notion.

The vocational ethos was a serviceable instrument for George Eliot, not only because it provided professional work with a higher sanction, but also because the anxieties and obstacles that faced the professional man were similar to those that faced the Puritan saint. His isolation and self-absorption in the solitary pursuit of his calling; the heavy responsibility for his own salvation; the mistrust of the claims of family and friends; the belief that any lapse in the methodical pursuit of calling can become a source of damnation — all of these shared features filled out a larger model which could encompass not only the promise of the new vocations but their anxieties and dangers as well.

George Eliot's recasting of the doctrine of vocation made it, in general, a disturbing paradigm of the anxiety of choice and freedom in posttraditional society. For Luther, the traditionalist, a man works out his calling in the place in which he finds himself. Everyone has a position, which is generally not of his choosing, and the coherence of the whole is guaranteed by God. In Calvin, the sovereignty of God and His election for each person similarly assures coherence. In the Puritanism of such a divine as William Perkins, however, the practical doctrine of vocation is more mediated. Although the relationship between man and his calling is part of a divinely appointed plan, a man can know if he has chosen correctly only by examining his own heart, by searching himself for a sense of fitness to the task, and above all by staying with it. The mobility introduced by the nineteenth century widened man's responsibility: the necessity of working at redemption in the station in which he found himself gave way to the responsibility of choosing that station. This was a different, and a more frightening, responsibility. In *Middlemarch,* it is true, there is the notion of a "natural difference of vocation," the idea that in the nature of things there is a right fit between a man and a calling which it is dangerous to ignore or deny. But a belief in nature (either upper or lower case) is ultimately only a tenuous means of mitigating the anxiety of choice and guaranteeing the coherence of the whole.

The new version of vocation, finally, permitted George Eliot to work out new strategies for the representation of fictional character. The refurbished idea of vocation allowed her to bypass the congealed conception of character in contemporary fiction, which most often explained personality in terms of such binary categories as egotism/compassion and mind/feeling, and to approach a more dialectical model of the personality. In the experience of vocation, selfish ambitions for personal distinction and selfless aspirations toward general amelioration are parts of a single matrix of desire. Similarly, the "intellectual passion" that is both the ambience and the propellant of vocational accomplishment is a single source for the exercise of judgment and knowledge on the one hand and the release of feeling and passion on the other. Because of its fundamental and fecund complexity, vocation as a fictional ethos brought within a single conception some of the major contradictions of the Victorian age.

2

THE SHAPE OF A LIFE IN BIOGRAPHY AND AUTOBIOGRAPHY

George Eliot's way of seeing character has its most conspicuous parallels among the great biographies and autobiographies of the mid-Victorian era. When a biographer rejects the leveling demands of biological time, he faces the question of how to render the shape of a life: where to begin it and where to end it and where to mark off its characteristic units. And when he rejects the nominalism that allows that an individual life fulfills only itself, the biographer is led to consider how the coming-into-being of that life participates in a larger, transpersonal pattern of meaning. For some of the great minds of the nineteenth century—for Carlyle, Newman, Mill, and Darwin—the idea of vocation, in the secularized form in which George Eliot also used it, provided a serviceable principle of biographical design. A life begins when the passion for a certain calling is first discovered, and it ends when that passion is consummated or spent, and between there are the moments of apprenticeship, trial, and production. How the story ends may be different in each case, but the shape of a life as a coming-into-vocation remains clear.

Eighteenth-century biographies were monuments of a different sort: part hagiography, forming and fixing the myth of an exemplary life; part revisionist enterprise, appropriating past figures on behalf of contemporary policies; part archive, selectively preserving documents and correspondence; part moral handbook, furnishing dicta and pronouncements to which readers might look for guidance in the conduct of their lives. The root desire to penetrate the mystery surrounding eminent lives was an impulse that could always be counted on. This eighteenth-century form became standard in the nineteenth century. "The exhibition of a person," Newman observed, "his thoughts, his words, his acts, his trials, his features, his beginnings, his growth, his end, have a charm to everyone." But while Newman was alive to the perplexities of beginnings, trials, and growth, these were not among the aspects of a life most often stressed by nineteenth-century biographers. In this respect Macaulay, the most popular and respected biographical essayist of the mid-Victorian era, carried on the mainstream tradition. Parentage and social origin interested him slightly; the maneuverings and triumphs of a public career interested him passionately; but the *process* whereby a seemingly backward and characterless lad like Robert Clive managed to grow up to become the founder of the English Empire — not at all. Macaulay wished to savor the power and paradoxes of the career and to avoid darker questions concerning the prices paid for its achievement.

Yet for some contemporaries who were less insulated than Macaulay from the energies of romanticism and the ravages of religious crisis, such questions could not be put aside. The self, with its persistent ambitions and disabling doubts, could not always be counted on as an inner ally, nor could the will be expected to operate independently from the feelings. Consider these passages:

The river of his History, which we have traced from its tiniest fountains, and hoped to see flow onward, with increasing current, into the ocean, here dashes itself over that terrific Lover's Leap; and as a madfoaming cataract, flies wholly into tumultous clouds of spray! Low down it collects again into pools and plashes; yet only at a great distance, and with difficulty, if at all, into a general stream.

Her finely-touched spirit had still its fine issues, though they were not widely visible. Her full nature, like that river of which Cyrus broke the strength, spent itself in channels which had no great name on the earth. But the effect of her being on those around her was incalculably diffusive.

The first is Carlyle from *Sartor Resartus* (1833), the second George Eliot from the "Epilogue" to *Middlemarch*.[1] Carlyle, in the guise of the editor of the autobiography of Diogenes Teufelsdröckh, has carried the narrative through his subject's student years, his experiments with a profession, and a tragic love affair up to a period of aimless wandering that precedes the despair of the Everlasting No. Here Teufelsdröckh's life faces a great existential chasm. Whereas conventional biographies, Carlyle seems to say, yield the gratification of viewing the steady consolidation of a life and its eventual entry into the broad ocean of public posterity, the reality of Teufelsdröckh's life allows no certainty. The leap he must take will unavoidably break the single linear flow of his life into a myriad of pools and rivulets that will empty into the ocean, if at all, only "at a great distance, and with difficulty." In the end, however. we discover that Teufelsdröckh has indeed come through; eventually he answers the Everlasting No with an Everlasting Yea, finds his true vocation, and enters the "general stream."

    This is not the case with Dorothea Brooke, whose story George Eliot concludes in the passage quoted above. Dorothea had once wished fully to commit her passionate nature to some great project on behalf of mankind, but because she is a woman she can act only through a husband. After a bad first marriage she marries an ardent public man whose good work for reform she furthers as the mother of his children and the keeper of his house. Unbroken, the accumulating force of her "full nature" might have won a great name in the world and perhaps even enshrinement in a respectable biography; but the river's strength had been broken, and the narrator takes it to be the job of the novel to trace the consequences of her life that do not show up on the public record: those "incalculably diffusive" effects, some of which nurture the lives of the primary creators of history and some of which are lost in the anoymous flow of family and daily living.

The fact is, biography is uninterested in the diffusive effects of an unhistorical life. If Teufelsdröckh had not successfully shot his Niagara, his life would not have been fit to write about. Not so with the novel. The subjects of biographies and the characters of novels face the same points of pressure in their histories: the emancipation from old creeds and the search for new ones; the interdictions of sexual role and the anxiety of occupational choice; the resistance of the world to individual achievement and the vanities of the self; the threats of romantic love and the entrapments of bad marriages. Yet, whereas figures in biographies always seem to come through and to secure achievements worthy of public discussion and description, figures in novels do not. They choose unwisely and become compromised and entrapped. But if novelistic characters stumble, their stumbling is always intriguing. The empathetic complicity that is the ground for our identification with the failures of the novel world is, moreover, a different and more complex bond than the admiration we feel for the "achievers" of biographies. The novel has the technical equipment to make unsuccess intelligible. It has the quality of intersubjectivity that biography cannot attain: the novel is not a "life" but an examination of interconnected lives.

What is important is the contiguity and overlap of the

two genres. For despite what it owes to the canons of its genre, *Middlemarch* in a sense can best be understood as emerging from a family affinity and from a family quarrel with biography. *Middlemarch* is an alternative to biography. The dominant tradition of the nineteenth-century novel may be concerned with ambition and aspiration, but not when those drives express themselves in work, vocation, and social usefulness. *Middlemarch* is special in this regard, for it has much in common with certain traditions of Victorian biography and autobiography.[2]

In the biographical tradition we are considering here the identity and nature of vocation are at issue. A career that consists of a progression of sentiments, opinions, and religious beliefs sets itself off from a career expressed through political action, public deeds, and scientific discovery. These two distinct biographical traditions, the biography of the spirit and the biography of achievement, both bear on George Eliot's work, and it is useful to examine them in this light. As examples of religious or spiritual biography, I take Carlyle's *Sartor Resartus* and Newman's *Apologia Pro Vita Sua*. The early Carlyle in his lectures on heroes and hero-worship provides examples of the biography of achievement, as do Smiles's *Lives of the Engineers* and Darwin's and Mill's autobiographies. (As is the case with surprisingly many of the contradictions of Victorian culture, Carlyle seems to be at the source of both conflicting traditions.)

The difficulties created by the spiritual biography are reflected in a digression by the narrator-editor of *Sartor Resartus*. In the necessary passivity of Teufelsdröckh's early education, we are told, one may detect the rudiments of a quality which the world will little understand in the grown man. "For the shallow-sighted, Teufelsdröckh is oftenest a man without Activity of any kind, a No-man; for the deep-sighted, again, a man with Activity almost superabundant yet so spiritual, close-hidden, enigmatic, that no mortal can foresee its explosions, or even when it has exploded, so much as ascertain its significance. A dangerous, difficult temper for the modern European; above all, disadvantageous in the hero of a Biography" (p. 81). Although Teufelsdröckh will grow up to become a great metaphysician, the author of a work on the philosophy of clothes which the present volume summarizes, celebrates, and explicates, to vulgar minds he has no real accomplishments and will therefore always be a "No-man" (p. 80). For the initiated there is an opposite problem: while Teufelsdröckh's abundant achievement may be properly valued, the medium of his activity is so spiritual that it simply cannot be registered. "Close-hidden" and "enigmatic," his active energies collect and explode, yet no mortal possesses the fineness of vision to anticipate the explosion or assess its significance. Empassioned by his German studies, Carlyle elsewhere in *Sartor* proclaims that thought is a "grand thaumaturgic art" and that an idea may exercise as revolutionary a force as any machine. Therefore, the education of the spirit, the progress and explosion of ideas, may be considered a true and sufficient subject of a life. But, as Carlyle himself realizes, such qualities of life are most "disadvantageous in the hero of a Biography!" (p. 81). It may be the truth, but how can it be told?[3]

Teufelsdröckh's story, as it is told in the second book of *Sartor Resartus,* begins as a collection of paper bags. The "Editor" receives from a Herr Heuschrecke six paper bags, labeled according to six signs of the zodiac. They contain "miscellaneous masses of sheets, and oftener Shreds and Snips" written in a scarcely legible cursive script. Although the slips are mostly fragments of wash bills, street advertisements, anecdotes, notes of dreams, and metaphysical treatises, occasionally intermixed are "autobiographical delineations"; from these scraps, undated and unconnected, the Editor pieces together Teufelsdröckh's career as best he can. Such a bizarre account of the origins of the final text, besides apologizing for Carlyle's distracted and digressive style, makes a statement about the difficulty of rendering such a "spiritual" life as Teufelsdröckh's and about the vast editorial organization—and audacity—needed just to make a start. A preponderance of editorial intervention is the price paid for getting the story told; the achievement of intelligibility cannot be left to the subject. A hybridization of conventions is necessary, the mixture of autobiography with biography, as if to say that neither the supposed authenticity of the subject's "I" nor the distanced authority of the chronicler's "he" is sufficient for the job at hand.

For Carlyle the paradox of spiritual biography consists in two facts: in literary terms, the life of the spirit cannot be written about unless it is translated into acts that form the narrative of a life; and, existentially, the spirit cannot achieve self-knowledge unless it is translated into outward works. "Know thyself" strikes Carlyle as a nearly impossible precept. It becomes partially possible only when translated into "Know what thou canst work at" (p. 132). Works are not only therapeutic or socially useful means of self-objectification, but ways in which the spirit becomes known to itself, ways in which the "inarticulate Self-consciousness" which dwells dimly within us can be rendered "articulate and decisively discernible."

Although it is not at first clear which sort of works can expedite this process, we find out immediately which ones cannot. Educated in a rational university permeated by "Profit and Loss Philosophy," Teufelsdröckh drifts toward the practice of the law. What calls him to his profession, we are told, and what keeps most young people from shifting from enterprise to enterprise until "they shift into their last enterprise, that of getting buried," is not the high call to vocation, but simply hunger. Professions, or as Carlyle calls them, "Bread Studies," have little to do with channeling one's energies in a chosen direction (p. 97). The energy mobilized by the professions resembles the circling of the gin-horse who contentedly fancies that he travels forward and forward while he moves round and round; he believes that by providing for himself he is contributing to the progress of mankind, whereas all he really adds to the world is "an additional horse's power in the grand corn-mill or hemp-mill of Economic Society" (p. 97). The professions, the worldly Puritan vocations, are a stultifying defense against the crisis of belief and originality; a man must break off this "neck-halter" before he can begin the search for true work.

True work cannot be found simply by consulting God or one's heart and hoping to choose the right path. True work is won by suffering, and the imperiled quest for it is the one true quest of life. The journey is attended by grave existential risks: Teufelsdröckh must divest himself of all secure cushions like "economic" professional work and face the prolonged ordeal of "No Object and No Rest." Teufelsdröckh's first station is actually a detour; he is detained on the Calypso-Island of romantic love where he falls in love with the beautiful Blumine, discovers the heavenly mystery of love, and enjoys love's joyful progress until the fateful dissolution of their love. The removal of this temptation is not Teufelsdröckh's doing, for Blumine allows herself to make a good match with a boorish and ignorant (though noble) wealthy young Englishman. Having given up his profession, Teufelsdröckh has renounced any tie between his genius and his ability to produce capital. His failure in love is thus forced upon him by his willing acceptance of his orphaned and disinherited condition.

Next, Teufelsdröckh takes up the pilgrim's staff and wanders around the world, encountering the novelty of new vistas and threading his way anonymously through all levels of society in all corners of the earth. "Hopeless is the obscurity, unspeakable the confusion" as he recapitulates the requisite course of sorrows trodden before him by Goethe and Byron. Sorrow turns into doubt, doubt hardens into despair. No far-flung wanderings can reverse the growing skepticism that began the first day of Teufelsdröckh's gymnasium education. If the universe is a machine, as he was taught, if man is ruled by his enviroment, if material happiness is the moral "calculus," then there is no room for hope, no place for faith.

Teufelsdröckh's "aimless Discontinuity," we are quickly assured, is but a "mad Fermentation" (p. 128). To begin with, though the underpinnings of his faith may have been worn away, he never allows the high tone of his conduct to lapse. God may have been idle since the first day of Creation, but Teufelsdröckh would never cease to regard Duty as a divine Messenger and Guide and to decry any notion of Duty as only a "false earthly Fantasm, made-up of Desire and Fear" (p. 130). Like many Victorians after him, the hero of *Sartor Resartus* is able to weather his crisis because of his belief in its divine source. Teufelsdröckh is saved, in addition, by clinging to the conviction that he is free and that no matter which mechanistic schemes of the universe threaten to consume this freedom, they are all nothing other than the Devil. With this act of repudiation, he is able to utter the protest of the Everlasting No. The posture of defiance sets his recovery in motion.

Teufelsdröckh's conversion is one of the best known things in Victorian literature: the Center of Indifference, in which he gazes upon the attainments of mankind: cities, handicrafts, tilled fields, roads, books, as well as war, gunpowder, and dueling; the annihilation of self and the triumph over the love of happiness; the Everlasting Yea with its empassioned commitment to selfless work within the "field of the actual." These three aspects of the conversion are especially relevant to the concerns of George Eliot's novels. First, the affirmation that work is meaningful is based on the renunciation of self. "The Self in thee needed to be annihilated" (p. 153). Like God's answer to Job, the secret revealed to Teufelsdröckh declares that man's happiness does not stand at the center of the cosmic mystery, and thus it is only as man renounces his demands to be served and accepts his duty to offer service himself that his humanity can be realized. In contrast to later notions of calling, which attempt to encompass both the ideal of service and the reality of ambition, the kind of work into which Teufelsdröckh is reborn is entirely self-forgetful. Second, there is the question of what particular work is worth doing. On the one hand there is the famous rhapsodic close of the penultimate chapter: "Produce! Produce! Were it but the pitifullest fraction of a Product, produce it in God's name! . . . Up, up! What so ever thy hand findeth to do, do it with thy whole might" (p. 157). Here only the act of production itself seems to matter, the reader being left to surmise that whichever of the Faustian labors mentioned earlier (fields tilled, swamps drained, bridges built) lies closest at hand would serve as well as another. But the one particular "divine calling" that becomes the hero's and that is held out above others is that of authorship. "By this Art, who so will may sacrilegiously degrade into a handicraft," Teufelsdröckh proclaims, "have I thenceforth abidden" (p. 159). So far from degrading art, Carlyle presents it as in essence the most active activity, the most powerful work, the most sacred calling. With Teufelsdröckh's discovery of the vocation of authorship Carlyle concludes the second book of *Sartor Resartus,* having attempted to solve the paradox of spiritual *biography* by having his subject be called to a form of spiritual *activity.*

Finally, there is the sense in which the biographical sections of *Sartor Resartus* are a kind of disappearing act. The Editor states in the last pages his strong suspicion that the autobiographical fragments are a fake, that in his "underground humours are intricate sardonic rogueries" which Teufelsdröckh has created as a deliberate mystification in order to protect the "citadel" of his private life. The Editor, however, is nonplussed: Teufelsdröckh's magnificent volume on the philosophy of work, which forms the remainder of the book, is safely in hand, and as long as he has the work, he is content to relinquish hope of sure knowledge concerning the life of the worker. Carlyle is having fun with the reader — the value of the biography is not vitiated. But the questions he raises about the ultimate relevence of biog raphy and its capacity to overcome mystification and inven- tion are questions that persist throughout the Victorian age.

The idea that telling one's story can involve manipulat- ing appearance and reality is exactly what is at issue for John Henry Newman in the *Apologia Pro Vita Sua* (1864).[4] For Newman the bond between belief and self is so organic that the story of his life can be presented as identical to the his- tory of his religious opinions. It is the integrity of this bond which Newman takes to be the point of Charles Kingsley's question, "What, then, does Dr. Newman mean?" Newman stands accused of believing one thing and professing an- other, that is, of being guilty of a gap between his opinions and his life. "Yes, I said to myself, his question is about my *meaning;* . . . He asks what I *mean*; not about my words, not about my arguments, not about my actions, as his ulti- mate point, but about that living intelligence, by which I write, argue, and act. He asks about my Mind and its Beliefs and its Sentiments; and he shall be answered" (p. 390). What we conventionally take to be the definitive achieve- ments of a life — words, arguments, actions — Newman insists are insufficient for the comprehension of the ultimate meaning of a life. Achievements and statements are only visible manifestations of a "living intelligence" that makes action possible. To ask what Newman means is not to ask for anything so limited as the interpretation of a particular doctrine (justified verbal misleading, for example) or partic- ular act (the delay in his conversion). The question of mean- ing is a question of mind: what sentiments are held with unwavering conviction, what beliefs assented to with perfect faith? He *is* what he believes, and his history is the story of the unfolding of his convictions. The rhetorical accomplishment of the *Apologia* lies in Newman's success in convincing us that the repudiation and espousal of sentiments and beliefs — entirely apart from any political or ecclesiastical consequences — are ultimate acts and that the attempt to render a written account of them is itself an act of extreme daring. "I have done various bold things in my life," Newman writes, "this is the boldest: and, were I not sure I should after all succeed in my object, it would be madness to set about it" (p. 93).

But if the matter of Newman's drama, like that of Carlyle's hero and the heroes of religious autobiographies, is spiritual and cognitive, the shape of that drama is different. There are varieties of conversion. Teufelsdröckh's abandonment of mechanistic doctrines for an embrace of the mystery of the universe is one model; the fall of numerous heroes of religious autobiographes from orthodoxy into tortured skepticism and then relaxed doubt (a "deconversion") is another. Newman's chief aim in the *Apologia* is utterly to disassociate his conversion from what the experience had come to mean in the nineteenth century: a violent revolution of mind expressed in a sudden movement from belief to unbelief (or in the opposite direction) or from one system of belief to another. Those conversions had been models of revolutionary disruption; his was one of development and progressive rationalization within the framework of belief. From the age of fifteen, when he first recalls having religious opinions, to the age of forty-four, when he was received into the church, Newman asserts that the degree of his religious faith did not alter, nor for that matter did the foundation of his doctrinal position. Early and late, during the Oxford movement and after, he has held by the importance of the dogmatic principle in opposition to Liberalism and by the particular doctrine of the reality of the visible church. Rome is the one issue that did alter. Until the last moment, Newman felt it was his duty as an Anglican clergyman to oppose conversion to Catholicism and to work for the rooting of his convictions within an English church that had been recalled to its first principles. But the refusal of that church to be recalled, along with the accumulating weight of positive proofs, eventually forced Newman to embrace Rome.

The fact that the *Apologia* ends with this event and begins at age fifteen suggests a peculiar relationship between writing and the life cycle that later finds strong expression in *Middlemarch*. Newman selects these years as the segment of his biological life worth evoking, explaining, and committing to writing. As to the beginning point: since the business of existence is the conduct of belief, life cannot be said to commence until convictions can first be consciously held; thus the meaningfulness of the early life—the gift of articulation through writing—is granted retroactively according to the achieved project of the adult life and is thought to "begin" only when serious convictions are first held.[5] (So Lydgate becomes known to us only from the moment he discovers medicine.) As to the point of closure, we have Newman's own statement: "From the time that I become a Catholic, of course I have no further history of my religious opinions to narrate. In saying this, I do not mean to say that my mind has been idle, or that I have given up thinking on theological subjects; but that I have no variation to record, and have had no anxiety of heart whatever" (p. 216). Newman's life requires explanation only as long as it remains at a distance from its final resting place. The justification for writing is therefore difference. His religious opinions are worth recording only while they are at variance with the church he is leaving and the church into which he has not yet been received. The Catholic church is an institution that by nature absorbs and restrains individual innovation in matters of doctrine. But reception into the church is only an extreme example of the point at which an individual project ends, either in capitulation or fruition, and thus ceases to matter for the purpose of writing—though the biological life goes on. (We "lose" Lydgate when he fails as a reformer and a scientist and becomes a conventional society doctor.)

In novels, characters with ambitious vocations are usually burdened with family problems. They cannot live their lives without spouses and cannot do their work with them; if the partner is not a perfectly suited helpmeet the character is fatally compromised in accomplishing his or her plans. Newman avoided such entanglements by remaining celibate, first by choosing the unmarried life of a fellow of an Oxford college and then by accepting the vow of chastity of a Catholic priest. As he presents his life to us, Newman is not vulnerable to the same needs as other men. At age fifteen he realized that it is the "Will of God" that he should lead a single life, and, except for a month or two during his twenties, he experiences no uncertainty on the matter. Newman resembles other men with high callings in that he has substitutes for biological fatherhood and brotherhood that are derived from his calling. For the guidance of his tutors and mentors at Oxford, for the gratifications of his relations with his own pupils, for the confraternity of the fellows, for the *esprit* of his coenthusiasts in the Oxford movement — for all this Newman feels the deepest gratitude and love; the scene of his leave-taking on the occasion of his reception into the church is suffused with genuine pathos. The *Apologia,* then, can meaningfully be read as the story of a passage between two surrogate homes: from the bosom of Oxford to the embrace of the church, the fellowship of the priesthood, and the society of the Oratory at Birmingham (though it is significant that the new home is beyond the plan of the work). Newman's success in establishing a serviceable family and home based on calling rather than biology is expedited by his single-mindness and his celibacy. Other men to whom renunciation comes harder and who attempt to form natural families and to undertake ambitious vocations find success considerably more difficult.

It is remarkable that just as we do not doubt for a moment the genuine selflessness of Newman's assimilation to his calling, a calling that formally requires humility and obedience, we are also entirely convinced of the irreducible sovereignty of his selfhood. As an undergraduate, Newman recounts, he never had the opportunity to meet John Keble, the author of the *Christian Year,* one of the most revered men at Oxford and later to be a strong influence on Newman. Newman later met him when he was elected to a fellowship at Oriel. Summoned to shake hands with the provost and the fellows, Newman maintained his composure until Keble took his hand, at which time he felt so "abashed and unworthy" that he wished he could sink into the ground. The anecdote, charming but ordinary, is accompanied by an extraordinary observation: "How is that hour fixed in my memory after the changes of forty-two years, forty-two this very day on which I write!" (p. 15). Here is a man with so hypersensitive an awareness of his personal history that his old age is permeated by precisely dated recollections from early manhood: a handshake remembered forty-two years to the day. Newman writes an account of his religious opinions which never allows us to forget that these opinions are *his* and not those of a movement: "I am giving my history from my point of view," he insists (p. 53). Quoting remarks he had made during the heyday of the Oxford movement, Newman claims that the Tracts were only the expression of individual minds and not intended as "symbols *è cathedrâ*": "individuals, feeling strongly, while on the one hand, they are incidently faulty in mode of language, are still particularly effective. No great work was done by a system, whereas systems arise out of individual exertion" (p. 39). Newman affirms the totality of his individuality, both effective and faulty, in an act of self-explanation that proceeds until the individual becomes coterminous with the system; at that point Newman continues to affirm but ceases to explain: his life in the church is not given to us. But if

Newman has effected entry into a system, we sense it as anything but a capitulation; rather, it seems like a deliverance from individuality that has been won painstakingly, step by step, as one closely argued set of proofs necessitates another. Conversion to Catholicism may mean absorption into the church, but Newman leaves no doubt about the degree to which he has been the author of his own conversion. His will has become identified with God's will, as George Levine has observed, but it has not been erased.

Various vocational heroes of fiction resemble Newman when they strive to be ambitious for the good, that is, to identify their personal ambitions with the interests of an idealistic goal or movement (or the other way around, which is most often the case). Fictional characters, however, rarely achieve complete identification, and it is their failure that makes them interesting. In biography there is always something left out of the telling: bad marriages, predatory love affairs, forgotten outcroppings of the soul. Such excrescences of the self are the field of the novel. What ultimately disappoints us in Newman is the tightness with which the circle of career is sealed. We hear nothing of the pride, temptation, and sin characteristic of the life of any religious man. We are denied access to anything but doctrinal matters and to none of Newman's postconversion years (before he wrote the *Apologia*), in which he suffered as an obscure and calumniated priest. Though he avers that his life as a Catholic has been one of "perfect peace and contentment," we persist in feeling that in his account of it we are denied a great deal.

In 1840, seven years after the publication of *Sartor Resartus,* Carlyle delivered a series of London lectures that, without departing from the fundamental insight of his earlier work, presented a new context for thinking about individual achievement. Teufelsdröckh's conversion had come to a climax in the realization that the world is alive with divine mystery rather than controlled by mechanistic necessity, and that a proper attitude of reverential obedience requires self-annihilating absorption in good works. Although in these lectures, *On Heroes, Hero-Worship and the Heroic in History,* Carlyle continues to affirm the divine mystery at the root of the universe, he introduces for the first time the possibility that special individuals might be chosen to be expressions of that mystery themselves and not merely self-forgetful vessels of it. Carlyle calls for the worship of that man who possesses a "free force direct out of God's own hand," the individual who is called to undertake the ambitious pursuit of historically significant action.[6] In drawing attention away from the inward drama of belief, Carlyle prepared the ground for a new literature whose preoccupation is the worldly exercise of ambitious calling.

The hero's relation of the mystery of the universe, according to Carlyle, is not one of obeisance but of articulation. What differentiates him from other men is his "sincerity," a quality that allows his actions to become a lens of such absolute transparency that the divine light of the cosmos passes through to mankind unobstructed. The divine mystery is one and eternal, and it is the hero who renders it articulate in the terms of a given age. It is he who distinguishes the essential from the unworthy and the godly from the idolatrous in the forms in which they become intelligible to a particular epoch. Although the higher truth he transmits is unchanging, the hero is invariably accounted an original man, because his message breaks through congealed usage and dogma and reintroduces the novelty of belief.

The role of the hero is also adapted to the age. In an age of paganism he will be a god, in the age of monotheism a prophet, in the age of Christendom a poet, in the age of religious corruption a priest-reformer, in the age of power a king, in the age of secularity a man of letters. By an intentional and insistent mixing of metaphors Carlyle does not allow us to forget that the heroic essence, like the mystery it expresses, is unchanging. Luther, the priest, possesses a "Kingly faculty" and serves as "the sovereign of this great revolution"; men of letters are a "perpetual Priesthood"; poets are aesthetic prophets, and so forth through virtually every permutation. Despite this seeming interchangeability, it is clear that Carlyle allows the man of letters to emerge as the unspoken object of his own hero-worship. Since articulation is the main job of the hero, it stands to reason that written language, rather than religious actions, should serve as the most transparent vehicle of expression. The age is marked by the succession of letters to the throne of religion; the great man of letters is now the Primate of England, "the writers of Newspapers, Pamphlets, Poems, Books, the real working effective Church," and literature itself the Scripture of a new age. The dissemination of writing by printing and the periodical press has also made literature the basic stuff of government: "Literature is our Parliament, too" (p. 164). In Carlyle's disproportionate elevation of the man of letters it is difficult not to be reminded of Teufelsdröckh's selfless dedication to the divine calling of authorship at the end of Book II of *Sartor Resartus*. Carlyle's man of letters, however, is a more ambitious creature who aspires to employ literature to reveal and legislate the truth of a new era, a truth equal to and expressed through his own will. Like a palimpsest, the sagelike figure of Carlyle himself shows through his portrait of the man of letters. Yet for all his praise of the exalted role of the man of letters, Carlyle can produce few concrete examples of literary heroes. Curiously putting aside a discussion of Goethe because of the impoverished "general state of knowledge about him," Carlyle is left with Johnson, Rousseau, and Burns, men about whom he can make only tepid claims. Johnson kept the light of truth burning in an idolatrous century; Rousseau's earnestness hardly offsets his morbid and excitable egoism; the great effect of the gracefulness and passion of Burns' gifts was that they drew admiration from both waiters and duchesses. It has been said of Carlyle that his habitual, frustrated melancholy arose in part from the fact that the events of his life were not large enough to match his heroic and tragic view of history; a similar disproportion can be noted in his inability to match his effusions about literary men with any historical examples. Carlyle saw in the rise of literature only its power. He failed to understand that the rise and dissemination of literacy might also be connected both to the closure of the possibilities for individual heroic action and the ascent of varieties of collective control.

After a miscellaneous education, abandoned experiments with the ministry, teaching, and the law, a spiritual conversion, immersion in German philosophical literature, and much rural isolation, Carlyle left the obscurity of Scotland at the age of thirty-nine for what was to become an ambitious and successful public literary life in London. Carlyle's heroes recapitulate in an idealized way the two principal movements of Carlyle's life. Before their entry into history, they lead lives of unassuming virtue. "All his 'ambition,' " Carlyle writes of Mohammed before his disclosure, "seemingly had been, hitherto, to live an honest life; his 'fame,' the mere good opinion of neighbors who knew him," (p. 54). Dante was a successful but ordinary magistrate, Luther a pious and obedient monk, Cromwell an industrious, Bible-reading farmer. In about his fortieth year, often after a period of contemplative withdrawal, the hero comes forth with a new message for mankind that is at first stated as a simple act of personal integrity. Mohammed sweeps away the idols, because they have become intolerable after his discovery that there is one God and He is All; Dante first sings to mitigate the anguish of exile; Luther says no to the perversion of Christianity embodied in the sale of indulgences; and Cromwell puts down his plough because *some-one* has to resist illegitimate authority. Within a short time the hero realizes that his act is only a first step in a lifelong mission whose scope is universal and historical. Thenceforth the hero embarks upon what is called in the case of Mohammed "the career of ambition"; convinced of the divinely revealed truth of his mission, he undertakes its propagation through conquest and polemic, that is, through the determined employment of the means of power.

Carlyle is at pains to define the true nature of his heroes' ambitiousness. He wishes to dispel the notion, especially in Cromwell's case, that there is anything intentional or calculating in the hero's earlier life. It is only when the hero enters the historical drama, Carlyle argues, that he ventures beyond zealousness for his private virtue; at that point Duty forces upon him an unwished-for responsibility to strengthen the hold of a larger idea. Once the "career of ambition" has been undertaken, Carlyle is eager to distinguish it from such seemingly similar careers of acquisition and aggrandizement as Napoleon's. Carlyle's stipulation concerns the fitness of a man to the task:

> there are two kinds of ambition; one wholly blamable, the other laudable and inevitable . . . The selfish wish to shine over others, let it be accounted altogether poor and miserable . . . And yet, I say, there is an irrepressible tendency in every man to develop himself according to the magnitude which Nature has made him of; . . . The meaning of life here on earth might be defined as consisting in this: To unfold your *self*, to work what thing you have the faculty for. It is a necessity for the human being, the first law of our existence. (P. 225)

There are few texts of the period in which the secularization of Puritan doctrines on vocation are more evident than in Carlyle's. God has been replaced by Nature, but there remains the essential congruence between the experience of being summoned by an outside agency and that of being impelled by an inner necessity. Although the same far-reaching aspirations and the same wide exercise of power that characterize the hero might be true of another man, if that man has not been chosen by Nature, then his ambition will be judged "wholly damnable"; he is not among the elect of Nature. Although they are not mentioned explicitly, one assumes that Carlyle also disqualifies those worshipers of Mammon, the great merchants and industrialists, who justified their own careers on the basis of the same dynamic identity of interests between the individual and God or Nature. Like George Eliot thirty years later, Carlyle carries over the Puritan doctrine of the vigorous prosecution of calling but drains it of its worldly, mercantile form and pushes it toward a more spiritual destination. What remains singular in Carlyle's teaching is the dramatic emphasis on the dire consequences of evading the duty to unfold the self. To fail to push that Nature-given potentiality for work and action to its outermost limit is to deny the very "meaning of life" and the "first law of our existence." That is not a small denial; the challenge to unfold the self at all costs is taken up later in the century and not only by men whose ambition Carlyle would have admired.

Carlyle had a monopoly neither on the designation of Victorian heroes nor on the definition of the heroic. In other quarters there was ready worship for great men whose impingement on history was somewhat less visibly momentous and whose entry into their vocation somewhat more natural. Throughout the second half of the nineteenth century Samuel Smiles produced a vast body of biographical literature concerning inventors, engineers, toolmakers, merchants, industrialists, and builders who, according to the degree of their contribution to the English nation and the degree of their "self-madeness," justly deserve to be accounted heroes of the age. Judging from the vast reception of Smiles's writings, the Victorian middle-class reading public did not disagree. The most ambitious of his works, both in terms of its historical scope and its aspiration toward authoritativeness, is *The Lives of the Engineers* (1861).[7] Just as earlier eras had celebrated their characteristic heroes in such works as *Lives of the Philosophers, Lives of the Poets, Lives of the Painters,* Smiles chose engineers to monumentalize as the great men of modern England, men like James Brindley, builder of the Duke of Bridgewater's and the Great Trunk canals; John Rennie, architect of three great London bridges, engineer of the Plymouth Breakwater and the London and East India docks; and Thomas Telford, designer and builder of the road network of modern Scotland.

What makes these figures heroic for Smiles is the intimate fit between their private careers and the larger mission of English civilization. Their technical genius was the genius of the age. The roads, canals, and bridges they built were part of the grand triumph of mankind over natural and geographic barriers. This is the same fitness between a man and his age celebrated by Carlyle; but whereas Carlyle speaks of a rapport between the will of man and the will of Nature, Smiles insists that nature itself must be broken and harnessed. The spread and improvement of inland transportation, to which most of these engineering feats contributed, expedited the development of sparsely populated regions and the accessibility of natural resources, creating the connections between markets and materials that made the Industrial Revolution possible.

In his own life the engineer is blessed by a further "fitness" between his work life and his personal life. Smiles's engineers do not experience a conversion point at which their calling is disclosed and their ambition radicalized and revealed to the world; from earliest boyhood they were fond of building things, using tools, and finding out how machines work, and this fondness naturally directed them toward apprenticeships to stonemasons and millwrights. When the opportunity eventually presented itself, they were ready to add their own genius and undertake unprecedented public works. Because the engineer's life is the continuous unfolding of one latent talent, biographical treatment can responsibly leave nothing out. Unlike Newman's selection of two points between which a life requires documentation, Smiles gives us biographies in which there is a complete overlap between work life and biological life. On his deathbed Brindley agrees to consult with a party of "eager canal undertakers" who had encountered a serious problem in the course of their work, and in another deathbed scene Rennie dictates letters to his assistants, urging upon them "attention, punctuality, and despatch."

Because there is no gap between work and life, not much can be said about the "personal life" of an engineer. Smiles appends to the end of each of his portraits a short chapter to satisfy his readers' curiosity concerning the "characteristics" of his subjects. We discover that his subjects generally have a wife and children (the fact is no more than stated), are even-tempered and law-abiding, orderly and disciplined, contemptuous of material acquisitiveness, and aloof from any sort of sensuousness. Smiles acknowledges the costs of professionalization and the ascetic regime it requires. In summarizing Brindley's character, he remarks:

> It is a great misfortune for Brindley, as it must be to every man, to have his mental operation confined exclusively within the limits of his profession. He thought and lived mechanics, and never rose above them. He found no pleasure in anything else; amusement of every kind was distasteful to him; and his first visit to the theatre, when in London, was also his last. Shut out from the humanising influence of books, and without any taste for the politer arts, his mind went on painfully grinding in the mill of mechanics. (P. 169)

Although for us these observations may be rich evidence of the harsh contradictions of vocation, for Smiles they suggest only a lamentable excess in an otherwise enviable career.

Because he does not fear the machine, he does not fear what would have been an anathema for Carlyle: that from over absorption in manipulating the machines that manipulate the world, man himself should come to resemble that mechanism.

In an apposite passage in his *Autobiography*,[8] Charles Darwin reflects on the years of his maturity: "Formerly pictures gave me considerable, and music very great delight. But now for many years I cannot endure to read a line of poetry: I have tried lately to read Shakespeare, and found it so intolerably dull that it nauseated me. I have also lost almost any taste for pictures or music . . . my mind seems to have become a kind of machine for grinding general laws out of large collections of facts" (pp. 138, 139). True to the scientific habit of mind that has created this condition, Darwin speculates that this "curious and lamentable loss of the higher aesthetic tastes" has resulted from the atrophy of those parts of the brain that were not exercised during the long years of scientific labors, and if he had his life to live again, he avers, he would try to forestall such decline by taking weekly exposures to music and poetry. The effort would be worthwhile, he says, for the loss of these tastes is a "loss of happiness and may possibly be injurious to the intellect, and more probably to the moral character, by enfeebling the emotional part of our nature" (p. 139). The cruel ratio between massive vocational achievement and aesthetic and emotional impotence (a dilemma that exercises John Stuart Mill in a different way) is a reality Darwin accepts with a sigh; it is a "lamentable loss" but one which he, like Smiles, thinks might have been avoided with a little foresight and a little self-restraint.

Darwin could never take the "injurious" potential of work too deeply to heart, because work gave him simply too much pleasure. Although he does not undervalue the stubborn application required by his scientific activity, Darwin emphasizes the fact that the story of his birth-into-vocation is the story of his choosing the path of life that promised the most passion and the most joy.

The picture Darwin presents of his early years is not endearing. As a boy he was fond of fibbing and taunting his friends and was unkind to animals. At school he was a failure at languages and generally considered a very ordinary boy "rather below the common standard in intellect." At Edinburgh, where Darwin was sent by his father to study medicine, Darwin lost interest in anatomical studies and slouched off altogether; of his subsequent years at Cambridge, Darwin writes that his "time was sadly wasted there," for he had fallen in with a sporting set and did not attend to his work. Two passions, however, give a dimension of interest to what is otherwise a characterless figure. One is Darwin's passion for collection. Among his earliest recollections are memories of foraging on the ocean shore for unusual shells and assembling and labeling the varieties of flowers that grew around his home. Collecting became an irrepressible urge. The only productive thing he seems to have done during his Cambridge years is to have amassed an impressive beetle collection and to have invented a novel means of obtaining beetles, which resulted in his identifying several new species. His other passion was for shooting birds. He became so "passionately fond" of shooting that he could not believe that "anyone could have more zeal for the most holy cause than I did for shooting birds" (p. 44). Although his summers were devoted to collecting, in the autumn his whole time was given up to shooting, usually at Maer, the estate of his uncle Josiah Wedgewood.

Darwin's love of shooting birds was gradually displaced by a passion for natural history. First, the nature of his collecting changed. Darwin had always been fired by the prospect of discovering new specimens and filling out his collection. He had never dissected his creatures, but toward the end of his Cambridge years, he was introduced to new developments in geology that explored the history of natural formations. He then realized that beyond mere classification lay unexplored reaches of comparative structure and historical origin, and thus collection gave way to investigation. (This same threshold between taxonomy and structure is at issue in *Middlemarch* between Lydgate and Farebrother.) After an August geological expedition to Wales with one of his professors, Darwin wonders at himself for having given up "the first days of partridge shooting for geology or any other science." Although his work as a naturalist on the *Beagle* requires immense attention to observing and recording natural phenomena, the older passion survived during the first two years of the voyage. But slowly a change occurs: "gradually I gave up my gun more and more, and finally altogether to my servant, as shooting interfered with my work, more especially with making out the geological structure of a country. I discovered, though unconsciously and insensibly, that the pleasure of observing and reasoning was a much higher one than that of skill and sport" (p. 79). From then on, Darwin fully arrives as a man of science and, despite his discoveries and his fame, remains essentially at one with his role.

Darwin, as he presents himself here, is a young Prince Hal whose penchant for amusement and sport eventually recedes in the face of serious responsibilities to a larger historical role; alternately, he is simply a man who learned to give directed and disciplined professional form to the spontaneous but inchoate fascinations of his youth. Whether as maturation or professionalization, a change has taken place which George Eliot would describe, as she does with Lydgate, as the discovery of an "intellectual passion" and the seizing of the "moment of vocation," a change that has the power to catalyze wayward energies into a new, generative identity. Becoming a man of science requires becoming a man capable of ascetic commitments to long voyages, to protracted and painstaking observations, to the arduous recording of his observations in writing, and to arguing them in books. It is difficult to conceive of Darwin's having undergone this metamorphosis if it had not been for an additional pressure. During his last year at Cambridge, Darwin's reading of such books as Humboldt's *Personal Narrative* and Herschel's *Introduction to the Study of Natural Philosophy* stirred up in him "a burning zeal to add even the most humble contribution to the noble structure of Natural Science" (p. 68). From then on Darwin is impelled toward vocational self-realization not only by passion for the work itself, but also by an ambitious desire to make some glorious contribution to the body of scientific knowledge and to "take a fair place among scientific men." Darwin stresses that he never went out of his course to achieve the popular fame that was eventually his; his ambition was for the approbation of such great men as Lyell and Hooker, who were also his friends. Like other scientific men, Darwin cared for the higher fellowship of scientists over all other relations.

Darwin's coming of age is signified by the union of the private self with a public task. The life of John Stuart Mill, however, as described in his *Autobiography* (1873),[9] is begun in its earliest moments with the inheritance of that union, a union that was the mature achievement of other men. His was not an easy inheritance; the story of his education speaks for itself. But that education did achieve its purposes—spectacularly. At the age of sixteen Mill was ensconced like his father in the service of the East India Company, leading an active life as a Benthamite radical. He helped to found the Utilitarian Society, where he debated the great issues of reform, studied the main texts of political economy with like-minded friends, and wrote on progressive political subjects for newspapers and journals. Mill's description of his happiness during those years of "youthful propagandism" is perhaps the classic statement of the happiness of a man fulfilled in his calling.

> I had what might truly be called an object in life; to be a reformer of the world. My conception of my own happiness was entirely identified with this object. The per-

sonal sympathies I wished for were those of fellow labourers in this enterprise . . . I was accustomed to felicitate myself on the certainty of a happy life which I enjoyed through placing my happiness in something durable and distant in which some progress might always be making, while it could never be exhausted by complete attainment. (P. 93)

Although Mill's statement is plain enough, several features are worth noting. (1) The object in life is poised at a point infinitely beyond the self and is related to the fundamental alteration of society. (2) Personal happiness is identified with the achievement of that object. (3) The needs for fellowship and sympathy can be sufficiently met by co-workers in the task (rather than by family, townsmen, coreligionists). (4) The object never ceases to demand gratifying allegiance, because by definition it can never be attained. The capacity of these features to work in concert is a function of their historical setting. During the heyday of reform in the 1820s agitation for progressive social causes resulted in a series of significant parliamentary measures, and these successes seemed to indicate that the nation would forever respond to enlightened influences. There was a body of doctrine (Benthamism) to support such efforts, societies of eager young men to encourage each other, and seemingly horizonless challanges to be met. These conditions in fact did not obtain forever, and although Mill's mental crisis and the subsequent adjustments in his life resulted from sources of personal dissatisfaction, he was also aware that irreversible changes in English life had fundamentally altered the conditions of subjective existence.

Two things are noticeably absent from Mill's statement. Although we would not hesitate to term Mill's desire to be a reformer of the world a commitment to a calling, Mill himself nowhere employs the vocabulary of secularized Calvinism in describing his life's work. Mill does not speak of himself as summoned by external sources of authority like

Duty or Society; his is an "object in life," a goal determined by and for himself.[10] Absent also is a concern for combining the pursuit of this object with earning a livelihood. Being a man without independent means, Mill had early on come to a willing acceptance of the separation between the kind of work that furthers ideals and the kind that pays an income and thus underwrites the remainder of one's activity. Mill found his duties at the East India Company, in addition to supplying him with generous amount of leisure, to be sufficiently undemanding to serve as "an actual rest from other mental occupations," and sufficiently intellectual not to be a "distasteful drudgery."[11] Because he held his ambitions solely to the sphere of moral influence and intellectual achievement — and thus renounced the honors and offices obtainable only with riches — Mill was able to keep his higher vocation insulated from the kind of threats and compromises to which it would have been vulnerable if it had had to serve also as a source of income.

The happy concert of these factors was disrupted when Mill put to himself a crucial question. "Suppose," he asked himself, "that all your objects in life were realized; that all the changes in institutions and opinions which you are looking forward to, could be completely effected at this very instant: would this be a great joy and happiness to you?" (p. 94). The answer was a resounding "No!" This question, if answered negatively, is fatal to any man of high ambitions; for if the gloriousness of the end is demystified, then the disciplined application to the means can no longer be counted on. Mill's negative answer derives from two sources: first, "an irrepressible self-consciousness" that refuses to allow him a naïve identification with the object of his work; and second, an equally irrepressible awareness of the existence of feelings that are not satisfied by the exercise of vocation and are worn away by the exercise of consciousness. The irony in Mill's dilemma is that precisely the tool that grants him success in his vocation — the habit and power of analysis —

becomes the weapon that destroys the singlemindedness necessary to pursue vocation. Self-analysis reveals that, apart from rationality, dimensions of affect and sentiment exist beyond the field of vocation, and they can never fully be brought in.

Mill tried very hard to incorporate them. After undertaking his therapeutic course of reading in Wordsworth, Coleridge, and Goethe, and after acknowledging the great role of feeling in human affairs, Mill sought to adjust his opinions to take account of these realities. As editor of the *London and Westminster Review* he published writers whose idea of progress was broader and more generous than the strict Benthamite rule. In his own writing Mill introduced the emotions as one among other postulates in the systematic explanation of human behavior. "When I had taken in any new idea, I could not rest till I had adjusted its relation to my old opinions, and ascertained how far its effects ought to extend in modifying or superseding them" (p. 110). In short, the economy of Mill's character as a whole was not transformed, nor was the essential mode of his reasoning nor the linear clarity of his writing.

An exception perhaps is Mill's long association with Helen Taylor and his eventual marriage to her. In Mill's description of her, she bears a striking resemblance to Dorothea Brooke (*Middlemarch* was published the same year as the *Autobiography*): a woman of sensitive nature and high intellectual tastes who was "shut out by the social disabilities of women from any adequate exercise of her highest faculties in action on the world without," and whose true value was not known beyond an intimate circle of friends. Helen Taylor attained the role Dorothea longed for but never achieved: a true helpmate to a worthy man of mind. Whether in historical terms Mill's account of their collaboration is overly loyal is irrelevant to the fact. Her portrayal in the *Autobiography* shows a woman who offered not only sympathy but also intellectual partnership.

Through this relationship Mill was able to restore a measure of the contentedness he had had before his mental crisis; Helen Taylor provided nourishment for the feelings of which he was newly aware and helped him identify once more with his calling.

The opening lines of the last chapter of Mill's *Autobiography* make an almost exact parallel to the lines quoted earlier from the same chapter of Newman's *Apologia:* "From this time, what is worth relating of my life will come into a very small compass; for I have no further mental changes to tell of, but only, as I hope, a continued mental progress, which does not admit of a consecutive history, and the results of which, if real, will be best found in my writings" (p. 155). Just as Newman asserts that the history of his religious opinions had been absorbed in the larger teachings of the church, Mill argues that his life can now be followed in his writings. Looking back on his life, he can state that in 1840 at the age of thirty-two his "mental changes" had passed; the extravocational factors that had disrupted his life had been taken account of, and there is therefore no longer a need for the extraordinary measure of autobiographical explanation. "I found the fabric of my old and taught opinions giving way in many fresh places," Mill writes of the period following his crisis, "and I never let it fall to pieces, but was incessantly occupied in weaving it anew" (p. 110). Mill regains his equilibrium as a weaver of opinions and finally passes himself to us in the form of his own artifacts.

3

MIDDLEMARCH: THE ROMANCE OF VOCATION

After describing the moment in which Lydgate first became conscious of a growing "intellectual passion" for medicine, George Eliot reflects on the treatment of vocation in literature.[1]

> We are not afraid of telling over and over again how a man comes to fall in love with a woman and be wedded to her, or else be fatally parted from her. Is it due to excess of poetry or of stupidity that we are never weary of describing what King James called a woman's "makdom and her fairnesse," never weary of listening to the twanging of the old Troubadour strings, and are comparatively uninterested in that other kind of "makdom and fairnesse" which must be wooed with industrious thought and patient renunciation of small desires? In the story of this passion, too, the development varies: sometimes it is the glorious marriage, sometimes frustration and final parting. And not seldom the catastrophe is bound up with the other passion, sung by the Troubadours. For in the multitude of middle-aged men who go about their vocations in a daily course determined for them much in the same way

as the tie of their cravats, there is always a good number who once meant to shape their own deeds and alter the world a little. The story of their coming to be shapen after the average and fit to be packed by the gross, is hardly ever told even in their consciousness; for perhaps their ardour in generous unpaid toil cooled as imperceptibly as the ardour of other youthful loves, till one day their earlier self walked like a ghost in its old home and made the new furniture ghastly. Nothing in the world more subtle than the process of their gradual change! In the beginning they inhaled it unknowingly: you and I may have sent some of our breath towards infecting them, when we uttered our conforming falsities or drew our silly conclusions: or perhaps it came with the vibrations from a woman's glance. (Ch. 15, p. 107)

Just prior to this passage, George Eliot describes how the inchoate intellectual energies of Lydgate's adolescence were suddenly catalyzed into a conscious passion for medicine, and presently she will proceed to describe how Lydgate managed to acquire a first-rate medical education by avoiding the English universitites in favor of more progressive centers of knowledge. In the meantime, however, she interrupts the work of description in order to address the reader in one of those remarkable instances of authorial disclosure that give *Middlemarch* its particular texture. Like a scientist pausing over his experiment to reflect on the general state of his discipline, the novelist looks up from her narrative long enough to deliver a meditation on the state of her art.

Literature, she concludes, is in serious trouble. An excessive preoccupation with romantic love on the part of both producers and consumers of literature has threatened the institutions of "telling" and "listening" with the prospect of exhaustion. How, we are asked in a series of tedious questions that mock their own tediousness, are we able to abide such repetition? Do we never weary of hearing stories of beauty and love, marriage and separation? Is it simply stupidity, or is there, perhaps, a quality of entropy fundamental to literature that tends toward diffusive excess and refuses to let go of a theme even after the experience and its literary representation have been emptied of meaning?

The answers are not important. The true task at hand is to reinvigorate literature by detaching it from a moribund preoccupation with romantic love and reconnecting it to the new, generative experiences of the age. Since the meaning of man's life in modern society has shifted decidedly from his relation to woman to his relation to the world, literature must now be induced to focus on the experience of work and vocation. The nobility of man's capacity for "generous unpaid toil," the promise of his commitment "to alter the world"—these must now become the writer's true subjects.

If this reorientation can be managed, the narrator continues, it will not dry up the flow of gratifications we expect from fiction. The play of passion and desire will still be there, even if the theme is vocation and not romantic love; for in the new age, a man's heart goes out to the world with a passion equal to his former longing for feminine beauty. This is not an incidental similarity, but a complete correspondence of function. The prospect of vocational achievement can lure the aspirant on with the same endowment of "makedom and fairness" as any woman's. Although it is only with "industrious thought and patient renunciation" that vocation can be won, like a beautiful woman, it too must be wooed. Vocation and romance converge later: "sometimes it is the glorious marriage, sometimes frustration and final parting," sometimes the gradual cooling of the ardour of youthful love. A man can fall in love with his vocational destiny, court it, and, in the end, marry with the same uncertainty of outcome that marks flesh-and-blood marriages.

There is, however, one significant difference between love and vocation, a difference that will require the new theme to be treated with a new set of imaginative instruments. Whereas the older art dilated on the intense early stages of the life of a marriage—on magnificent attraction and glorious union—the new art must necessarily focus on the stages of disillusionment and breakdown. Even the nature of the separation is different. Although the union of a man and a woman comes asunder with the melodrama of fateful parting, a man's separation from his vocation is marked only by an imperceptible weakening of resistance to the forces that would shape him "after the average." "Nothing in the world more subtle than the process of their gradual change!" One day a man awakes to find that his passionate commitment to vocation has cooled and conformed, and he knows not how or when it happened. Since the new fiction will have to register the subtle processes of winding down and giving in, it will have to employ techniques capable of a finer concentration on the gradual changes that mark the movement from one stage of life to another. If in the past the grand moments of passion could comfortably be the writer's subject, the establishment of vocation as the modern theme will require closer measurement of more complex experiences.

In this text from an early section of *Middlemarch,* George Eliot reveals a program for the novel of the future, the novel of vocation. Living in one of the great moments of historical discontinuity (the Middle Ages of the Troubadours and the Renaissance of King James are conceived of as a vast, undifferentiated stretch of time that has given way to the modern period), the novelist stands before the necessity of appropriating for writing the central experiences of the new age: work, vocation, and the passion to improve the world. We need not read the manifesto of the novelist as a summary of the meaning of novel, or, for that matter, as an indication that an example of the new novel has been produced. Yet as a declaration of authorial intent, the text is important, for to read *Middlemarch* is to watch the writing itself both respond to and swerve away from the conscious will of the novelist. And at the very least, we are introduced to recurrent concerns that determine the shape of the novel.

To begin with, we can expect the constellation of experience that includes erotic love, marriage, children, and family to have an altered value in *Middlemarch*. Although the formation of new families was once a central event of the novel as a genre, here it has been decidedly moved to the margin; as for children, *Middlemarch* is a consummately adult world in which the experiences of childhood and youth barely figure. Although erotic love, that "passion sung by the Troubadours," continues to play a role in the novel, it persists chiefly as a demonic presence, a "catastrophe" that wrecks the more valuable marriages of men to their vocations.

In addition, we expect *Middlemarch* to be a world in which man's new means of realizing himself will be his own works. If in the past a man could realize himself by occupying a position in society that required him to do nothing in particular—a gentleman being a man who could afford not to work—the modern era will see men judged by the works, beyond land and children, they leave behind them. No longer merely a compromising struggle for livelihood, work has been transformed into an impassioned struggle to change the world.

Since value is so firmly rooted in significant work, the special anxieties of the novel's characters are for the success of their vocational projects: fears of incompletion, insignificance, interference, and incapacity. Since, moreover, the completion of his work is something for which the individual alone bears full responsibility, the attendant anxieties must also be endured alone, removed from the consolations of family and fellowship.

Finally, and perhaps most essential to the nature of *Middlemarch,* is the fateful intertwining of vocation with originality and negation. To work means to assert one's individuality, to mean to "shape [one's] own deeds," to strive to effect an original relationship to the world. Since the world with its routinizing and collectivizing pressures repels such efforts, vocation can proceed only through acts of resis-

57

tance and negation. Furthermore, since the "world" is nothing other than the community we all inhabit, it is our own sense of security that is unhinged by our vocational assertion. And just as we find ourselves threatened, we also constitute a threat to others in the form of a series of temptations we present to young aspirants. "You and I may have sent some of our breath towards infecting them, when we uttered our conforming falsities or drew our silly conclusions." Communal opinion and that older passion, "the vibrations from a woman's glance," will dog the steps of the characters of *Middlemarch,* hampering the free and full exercise of vocational expression.

One of the hallmarks of *Middlemarch* is that its narrator, as a figure in the novel, is also touched by these contradictions. For if narration counted for anything in the eyes of both the historical Marian Evans, the author of the novel, and George Eliot, its narrator, it was most certainly as a vocation. And like other vocations, narration realizes itself through negation: the delapidated stage props of romantic love have to be cleared away before the real drama of modern life can be portrayed. To write means to transform the world of literature, as other men transform the social world, by negating superseded forms and originating new fictions.

The problem of originality and community are imbedded in the rhetorical complexity of the text quoted above. The voice that speaks throughout speaks as a "we," presupposing a community of sentiment and an identity of condition. We *all* persist in tolerating endless stories of romantic love; we *all* decline interest in that other kind of "makdom and fairnesse"; it is the exhalations of *our* breath and the "conforming falsities" of *our* opinions that fatally infect the aspirant to vocation. Yet beneath the communalizing sweep of the "we," the voice that addresses us is essentially polemical, encouraging resistance to discredited ideas and soliciting approval for new undertakings. As readers, we cannot so easily be collapsed into the seamless solidarity of the speaker's "we," for we know that we are being spoken to, and spoken to for a purpose. The consciousness of being the object of a rhetorical strategy consequently makes us wonder whether the "we" is a sign of achieved community or, perhaps, enforced collectivization. The drama of *Middlemarch* unfolds in precisely these spaces that separate the questioning individuality of the reader (or character) from the generalizing will of the narrator (which is itself divided). Individuality and individuation are part of the idea of vocation, and in their resistance to the embrace of community we find the ironic pain that defines the world of the novel and animates its story.

Whether George Eliot in the end succeeds in making *Middlemarch* the new novel about the new theme is far from certain; but that the idea of vocation permeates the novel cannot be denied. In considering Fred Vincy's future, Caleb Garth remarks to his wife, "Fred says frankly he is not fit for a clergyman, and I would do anything I could to hinder a man from the fatal step of choosing the wrong profession" (ch. 40, p. 296). Choosing the wrong profession can be an unfortunate prospect and the cause of much unhappiness, but is it fatal? The word takes the already earnest tone of Caleb's remark to an ultimate level and lets us know that nothing less is at stake than spiritual life and death. Somewhat further on, Fred becomes melancholic about the responsibility of choosing an occupation, and he tells Mr. Farebrother that if Mary Garth will accept his love he will leave the choice up to her. "That is nonsense, Fred," replied Mr. Farebrother. "Men outlive their love, but they don't outlive the consequences of their recklessness" (ch. 52, p. 377). Again we are in a world of transvaluations: the eternal redemption or loss that was thought to have hinged on winning the woman of our desires is nothing compared with the consequences of a reckless choice of profession.

This is not just Fred's predicament. Everyone in the

novel is somewhere along in the process of making a decision about vocation or living with the "fatal" consequences of his choice. In Casaubon's desperate obsession with authorship we see the appalling end of the line; in Will Ladislaw's quixotic flirtations with art and politics we see its hopeful beginnings. Since before the novel gets underway Lydgate has already met and submitted to the "moment of vocation," it is in his losing struggle to remain faithful to his marital commitments — both to medicine and to Rosamond — that he comes most fully alive. Even the characters who receive less attention than the major figures give evidence, usually in the distant past, of having undergone a fateful encounter with vocational destiny. Mr. Farebrother, because of family responsibilities, had to forgo his passion for natural history and enter the clergy; Caleb Garth had gone into the building business on his own for a time, but, having failed, returned to working for others as an estate agent; Bulstrode stopped his ears to a call to the dissenting ministry and took advantage of a momentary opportunity for a life of corrupt prosperity; and, of course, Mr. Brooke, the novel's emblem of childish irresponsibility before the task of occupational choice, seems to have repeatedly postponed the moment, having one time or another "gone into" almost everything. Ironically, the character who stands firmly at the symbolic center of the novel has no profession whatever. As a woman, Dorothea is not allowed the direct access to the world possible for men. Despite this fact, what she wants most in life is to do some great good for the world, and although there is no adequate vehicle for this desire, it remains in George Eliot's eyes unequivocally vocational. The impossibility of its satisfaction does not change its nature. In fact, Dorothea's womanhood, instead of being an anomaly, is simply the most extreme example of the variety of constraints and contingencies that frustrate the urge to alter the world. The intensity of her desire and the impossibility of her situation make Dorothea a kind of symbolic origin in relation to which the members of the crowded cast of *Middlemarch* locate themselves.

VARIETIES OF ASPIRATION AND GOODNESS

Although the theme of vocation is not dealt with directly or extensively in George Eliot's earlier fiction, it is present in an oblique way, and its treatment reflects the transition from traditional to antitraditional ethics described by Weber. In *Scenes from Clerical Life* there is little interest in the work people do outside the clergy, but the workshop and the dairy in *Adam Bede* become important symbolic settings. Direct contact with the materials of nature and the struggle to render them useful for man define Adam's work as a carpenter; he transcends and fulfills himself by producing objects that are the direct results of his own labor. Arthur Donnithorne's life, precisely because it has no basis in direct labor, results in a series of self-indulgent and irresponsible acts. Although it is easy to recognize in Adam's earnest and unambitious work the kind of economic activity described by Weber's traditional type, the fact that as a character he is so insistently idealized indicates that the author has already traveled some distance from a concern with the particularities of the experience. Dorlcote Mill in *The Mill on the Floss* is of a piece with Adam's workshop, but its eclipse by the commercial world of the Dodsons is so irreversible that it can no longer even be idealized: like Maggie's childhood, the "golden gates" have closed behind it, allowing it to be evoked only with nostalgia. The Dodsons and the grown-up Tom, with their unswerving self-discipline and self-confidence about the value of their calling, clearly live a life of capitalist asceticism. It is left to Maggie to incarnate in her misery and disorientation the unfulfilled needs of affection, imagination, and sensibility that were among the chief costs of the increasing rationalization of economic life. Something in Maggie's need for affection seems like a desperate substitute for some more outward, worldly expression. "She wished," George Eliot writes of her, "she could have been like Tom who had something to do on which he would fix his mind with a steady purpose, and disregard everything else."[2] The consciousness that the unavailability of a fixed purpose is related to sex is very much there. When Maggie says to her brother, "you are a man, Tom, and have power, and can do something in the world," Tom replies, "Then if you can do nothing, submit to those who can" (bk. V, ch. 5, p. 365).

With *Felix Holt* there arises a new and conspicuous presence in the world of the novels: the individual of immense will and passion who yearns to do some great good for the world. The figure is anticipated in Dinah, the Methodist preacher of *Adam Bede*. Unlike most of the characters of the early novels whose desires touch the brother, squire, or lover near at hand, Dinah preaches to the world community and appeals to the souls of all Christians. Although she eventually becomes a mother and permits the domestication of her passion, the procession of men and women with great projects for the world does not stop with her. In a different setting but in much the same spirit, Felix Holt appeals to the hearts of workingmen everywhere to educate themselves and to make worthwhile use of their new freedom and opportunities. Felix is, in every sense, a man with a mission, a man who has been called, a man entrusted with a sacred task. Although he establishes and clarifies a new pattern, he fails as a fictional character, and *Middlemarch* in a sense places his corpse beneath the lens of empirical observation and begins to explain the reasons for death. In *Middlemarch* the vast and inchoate yearning for the good is broken down and redistributed among the multitude of fictional forms that populate the novel. George Eliot's novelistic career ends with an attempt to recombine the fragments into a single, towering figure. Bearing the weight of so massive an intention, Daniel Deronda becomes a kind of speaking vision, whose message is unmistakable: answering the call is the most glorious of human possibilities.

These characters share many of the features Weber attributed to the new economic man: a natural individual talent, the sense of having been called, the belief that one's work in the world serves a higher purpose, acceptance of responsibility for the affairs of the world as a trust or stewardship, the interpretation of success in the world as a sign of election or salvation, the drive to achieve ever more and more. Even given these similarities, however, the essence is missing: the yearnings of Felix, Dorothea, and Daniel have nothing to do with money. In order to restore to vocation its authority, to renew the health of the social life, and to reverse the exhaustion of the novel, vocation would have to be purged of its contamination by capital. The kind of vocation George Eliot has in mind involves the disciplined accumulation of ambitious good deeds rather than material goods or capital. Once vocation as a way of being in the world was sufficiently purified, it could receive a new essence drawn from contemporary philosophies of amelioration. Will and Mr. Brooke scheme to correct abuses and to effect such fundamental structural reforms as the extension of the franchise. Lydgate, too, is committed to reform, though only in the limited sphere of the medical profession. He has an additional enthusiasm: he is enthralled by the prospect of scientific discovery and the possibilities it offers for relieving human misery. The various faces of benevolence appeal to Dorothea, Bulstrode, and Sir James Chettam; talk of model farms, model hospitals, colonies of workers' cottages, and scientific farming runs throughout the novel. The rhetoric of social hopefulness is everywhere; one cannot turn a page without reading of notions, schemes, reforms, and plans. After Casaubon's death, for example, Doeothea firmly rejects the idea of remarrying and announces her intention of establishing and supervising a model workers' colony. Celia is disappointed that her sister will not undo the mistakes of her first marriage by this time marrying "blood and beauty," but she manages to reply with a largesse that characterizes the novel as a whole:

"Then you *will* be happy, if you have a plan, Dodo," Celia says, holding up her baby, "perhaps little Arthur will like plans when he grows up, and then he can help you" (ch. 55, p. 401).

Philanthropists and reformers abound in Victorian fiction, but George Eliot's use of them is distinctly her own. Dickens is the other great artist of the good, and measured against his representations of the energies of benevolence, the cast of *Middlemarch* comes most into its own. To begin with, the objects of charity in the work of each author differ considerably in scope. Pickwick, Mr. Brownlow, the Cheerybles, John Jarndyce, Boffin, and Garland shower their gifts on those particularly fortunate souls who happen into their lives, on relations and on strangers who usually turn out to be relations. The benevolent gaze of George Eliot's characters, however, is directed toward the horizon, and they seek to improve nothing less than a village or a class or a profession or the world itself. (The story the novel has to tell, interestingly enough, is how these ambitions are taught to give way to the more modest opportunities for good that lie, like the Dickensian circle of recipients, unexpectedly close at hand.) In addition, one of the main "symptoms" of Dickens' benevolence, as Humphrey House puts it, is "generosity, in money and in kindness, which costs nothing,"[3] and indeed the Cheerybles and Mr. Brownlow seem to have a limitless supply of psychic and fiscal resources. In *Middlemarch,* however, what distinguishes the real acts of giving from self-gratifying "plans" is precisely the pain and sacrifice that attend them. As each selfless act exacts its pound of flesh, we are meant to see that there is nothing accidental about this kind of payment. Finally and perhaps most importantly, Dickens' philanthropists very much *are* their philanthropy, enjoying a fortuitous unity of character, deed, and disposition. "They are all good-*natured*," House points out, "and seem to act as they do because they cannot act otherwise."[4] In this respect, if the figures of George Eliot were translated into the Dickens world, they would appear most alien. For them the good is an ambitious yearning whose fulfillment is blocked and whose origins are problematic. Rather than effortlessly desiring the good, their strivings are driven by personal need and by the hope of personal redemption. They continually come up against the problem of matching the self with its destined vocation, the resistance met by the vocational project at the hands of the social medium, and the necessity of being reeducated about the true nature of the good.

However divergent the worlds of the two novelists may seem, Dickens creates a matrix of attitudes out of which the work of the later writer emerges. Work, for Dickens, means the methodical application of self to the world in the responsible spirit of stewardship. Although Dickensian characters may not apply themselves for the purposes of glory and distinction, they nevertheless exist through and because of this application. Success no longer depends on inherited status and resources; with the right set of values they can arrive, regardless of their class. It is a career open to virtue.

Middlemarch is our best source for understanding the noninstitutional aspects of the impulses toward reform, benevolence, and scientific discovery that illuminate the 1830s and 1840s. While one would look to the Blue Books, or to the Parliamentary debates on the Factory Acts, or to the accounts of Owenite communities for an institutional history of the various schemes of improvement, it is to George Eliot's novel that one must look for their "natural history,"[5] that is, their origin in the self and their growth in the social medium. The particular histories of Dorothea, Lydgate, Will and—in a perverse sense—Casaubon tell us much about how the private self is interwined with the public task. The hungers that overshadow the commitments, the disguised religious needs that seek new altars, the expectations that become the fuel for movement itself, the momentary seizure of the task by the self—all these betray a preoccupation with the origins in the particular self of the ideas and institutions that shape the larger culture of man. As to their further development, *Middlemarch* is the locus classicus for the study of the fate of individual projects in the "embroiled medium" of the social life. The novel records with finely calibrated notations how the desire for the good responds to the "small solicitations of circumstance" and how it holds up against the opinions of the community, the exigencies of livelihood, the usages of custom, and entanglements of love and marriage, and the solicitations of power. Moreover, the novel reverses the perspective to show us, from the point of view of the community, the heavy social costs of individual desire. That Lydgate's insistence on reform and Dorothea's self-gratifying benevolence disturb the life of the community and tamper with the welfare of its members indicates how much vocation is an individual act that has the community as its dialectical opposite.

HIGH SANCTIONS AND LITERARY SOURCES

Although Victorian fiction deals variously with the general division of labor, with the professions, and with the anxieties of job choice, it is not until *Middlemarch* that the peculiar experience of vocation, with its religious origins, receives serious fictional treatment. Why is that so? Or, to ask the question another way, why did it happen at all? A speculative answer to these questions might be offered along the following lines.

Two things, let us say, join to make up the experience of vocation: the disciplined energy of the self and the commitment to end beyond the self. Despite the anxiety that accompanied the struggle to achieve the certainty of salvation, the Puritan saint at least had in the idea of salvation a supreme goal capable of giving value to even the severest and most banal forms of energetic labor. However, as a result of the secularization of consciousness in the next two hundred years, this sense of elevation and authority was eroded, and thus the fit between vocational energy and vocational sanction became increasingly difficult to maintain. Although during the nineteenth century more men worked with more zeal than ever before, the ends that gave meaning to their labors, when they were not unabashedly forms of self-interest, were vague slogans such as "Progess" and "the Good of All," slogans that patently lacked religious authority. One of the functions of fiction at this time was to record the effects of the resulting vacuum and to disclose the disfigurement of work in a world in which ambition must ultimately be self-regarding. Fiction becomes concerned not only with the egoist's greed, but also with the man of good will and his frustration in finding an adequate analogue in the universe for the breadth of his desire for individual achievement.

In the case of George Eliot, the situation is otherwise. Writing of a period forty years before her own, she fabricated a fiction of an era on the eve of reform in which men could still be nurtured by a sense of social hopefulness. In the world she created the professions had not yet become entrenched, reform was confident of its power to abolish abuses, science had not yet revealed the more frightful secrets of nature, and benevolence still hoped to ameliorate the moral condition of the poor and the heathen. Though not supernatural, these "causes" served nonetheless as ends idealistic enough to give dignity to individual enterprise — and thus apparently to restore vocation as a model for the authentic activity of a life. Such restoration (which made vocation a sufficient and attractive model for the organization of character) was not stable, however. George Eliot wrote knowing that the possibilities for exalted action in the late 1820s would soon be foreclosed. Given this prospect, there were three outcomes possible for her characters: demoralization and capitulation to a world in which ambition can never transcend itself; the renunciation of personal ambition, a course leading to rebirth into an invisible or nonexistent community of moral reciprocity; and the elevation of ambition beyond society into pure messianic transcendence. These are the directions taken by Lydgate, Dorothea, and Deronda, respectively.

The literary sources for the construction of an ethos of vocation, consequently, could come only from literature and eras that offered similar examples of high sanction for individual endeavor. Judged by this standard, the novelistic tradition of England, George Eliot's immediate patrimony, was inadequate; it was necessary to reach farther back to periods when the ends of action, its *telos,* were authoritative and empowering. One such model was the prophet of the Hebrew Scriptures. Abraham, Moses, Samuel, and Jeremiah were men who had been summoned from obscurity and entrusted with a sacred mission. The prophet was special, not because he possessed more holiness than other Israelites, but simply by virtue of the task God had thrust upon him. As in a vocation, his prophetic career began at the moment of choosing, which for the prophet was an experience of being chosen rather than one of free election. The essence of his task was negation and reformation; he was called to denounce the complacency of the people and to exhort them to return to their obligations under the divine convenant. Having no coercive power of his own, the prophet relied on the force of symbolic action: he appeared in the marketplace in sackcloth and ashes to warn of the impending destruction; he paraded weighed down by an ox yoke to demonstrate the consequences of an alliance with Egypt; most of all, like the novelist himself, he relied on the mysterious power of language to engender belief and alter behavior.

The Gospels and the Fathers present a different type of the summoned man: the man whose originating experience is his conversion. Paul, on the road to Damascus to persecute Christians, is an example of a man whose conversion overtakes him as a sudden and total reorientation of his beliefs and personality.[6] Augustine, on the other hand, is an example of a man who approaches the truth at the end of a long quest; yet no matter how conscientiously he prepares himself (Augustine studies Neoplatonism and attends Ambrose's sermons), he cannot be converted to the spiritual life without the final, unpredictable intervention of grace. If prophecy is a model for the moment that inaugurates the vocational careers of the male characters in the novel, then conversion is the model for the turning point in the development of female characters at the conclusion of the novel. Esther Lyons in *Felix Holt,* Dorothea Brooke, and Gwendolen Harleth lead lives of varying degrees of striving and egotism until they are granted moments of vision at the ends of the novels (for instance, Dorothea's all-night vigil at the end of chapter 80) in which they glimpse the larger life of humanity and their humble place in it. Although these women are in every sense reborn into a new community of faith, their conversions take place just as the novels are ending; their new lives spread into a shadowy extraterritorial space beyond the bourn of fiction.[7]

George Eliot's wide reading in Greek epic and medieval romance also contributed heroic materials to the ethos of vocation. Lukàcs has pointed to this literature as a source for the fact that in the historical novel the hero's childhood and adolescence are not often described; the hero reveals himself (and is revealed by the writer) only at the moment when his life becomes meaningful in terms of the larger social world, that is, when he accepts or declares his mission.[8] Lydgate's conflict within himself and with the other medical practitioners of Middlemarch is a version of the hero's *agon,* yet, as in the ironic displacement of this myth, instead of rebirth or recognition his career ends in disintegration and disappearance. Like Orpheus, his fate takes the form of *sparagmos* or tearing to pieces: the final dismantlement of Lydgate's ambitions and integrity.[9]

The most important literary source for the idea of vocation is the great writer of the culture that originated the institution: Milton. Although after taking his degree at Cambridge Milton declares that he has chosen poetry instead of law (*Ad Patrem*), he shows in poems like Sonnet VII ("How Soon Hath Time") his anxiety over having nothing to show for the disproportionately long duration of his studies. The period of his self-preparation is no ordinary apprenticeship but a sign of the dedication of a Nazarite to the perfecting of his service of God. This is an "inward ripeness" that can be furthered by diligent application but finally brought to maturity only by God's providence. Milton's release from his apprenticeship, his readiness to reveal "that one talent which is death to hide," is recorded in *Comus* and *Lycidas*. *Comus* is a deliberation on whether virtue needs celibacy to sustain it, or whether, as it is finally determined, an inward conviction of chastity is enough to protect the poet as he enters society. Similarly, although *Lycidas* begins with the sense that the poet has been called upon to sing at a time when his talents have still not ripened enough to warrant fame, the poem concludes with the certain conviction of reward and immortality. Ultimately, Milton makes the passage from "the vague poetic inclinations of one intended for the ministry . . . to the dedicated poet's conviction that his art was more a sacred service than any other."[10] For Milton the poetic vocation becomes not merely a discharge of obligation to God but an instrument of prophecy through which the world might be redeemed for God. As other Puritan saints did in regard to the secular vocations of commerce, politics, and the magistracy, Milton spiritualized his calling, the secular vocation of writing.

The vocational preoccupation of George Eliot's late novels is with the labors of its author as much as with those of its characters. Although the vocational endeavors of the major characters of *Middlemarch* are all shown to be flawed, the implied figure of the novelist emerges as the novel's one "worker" whose enterprise succeeds. The re-

demptive power of her vocation, the sense that its exercise
not only actualizes herself but redeems others (from isolation, misunderstanding, egotism) is, I believe, a Miltonic
legacy. Although the centrality of the novelist-artist remains
half hidden in George Eliot, in the later fiction of the cen
tury it moves clearly to the center of attention, finally establishing itself as the supreme and sovereign subject of literary
representation.

4

MIDDLEMARCH: ORIGINS
AND TAXONOMY

$$W$$ hen the "moment of voca-
tion" overtakes Lydgate he is still an adolescent of promiscu-
ous intellectual curiosity. "It was said of him, that Lydgate
could do anything he liked, but he had certainly not yet
liked to do anything remarkable" (ch. 15, p. 106). For the
boy of "ready understanding" and "vigorous animal" energy, it requires the chance perusal of an encyclopedia
article on anatomy to bring these forces to bear on one object. Like metal filings exposed to a magnet, Lydgate's ran-
dom energies assume a shape that becomes the ordering
principle for his life's work. Paying special attention to this
process, Weber describes the importance Puritan writers
attached to choosing a certain and "well-marked" calling
because of its power to organize man's activity. Without a
certain calling, a man "lacks the systematic methodical
character which is . . . demanded by wordly asceticism."[1]
Now that Lydgate's life proceeds within a calling, the narrative tests the temper of his asceticism, that is, the degree to

which the organizing power of the calling succeeds in securing itself against outside forces that threaten total commitment to the work.

Apprenticed to a country practitioner, Lydgate is determined not to settle for a makeshift medical education of this sort, or, for that matter, to be drawn into a conventionally successful career that would take him from the "expensive and highly-rarified" instruction of Oxford and Cambridge to a plush London practice and the prestige of the Royal College of Physicians. From the beginning he pits his own talent and desire against usage, fashion, and guild-exclusiveness by attaching himself to the advance guard of science. Pursuing his studies in London, Edinburgh, and Paris, where medicine is more of an experimental science than a drug-dispensing trade, he follows the development of the lastest procedures and performs experiments of his own. When he is ready to return to England, Lydgate has before him an ambitious set of plans that involve overcoming the "irrational severance" of pursuits that had bedevilled his predecessors (ch. 5, p. 108). He would combine the then-separate functions of medical doctor and surgeon, thus coupling diagnostic expertise with technical skill and anatomical exploration. Also, he would combine a lofty intellectual passion for medicine with a warm, personal concern for the people he attends. "He cared not only for 'cases,' " we are told, "but for John and Elizabeth, especially Elizabeth" (ch. 15, p. 108). Clearly, Lydgate's most ambitious project is to marry scientific pursuit to professional enthusiasm. The careful and useful clinical work he performs in Middlemarch, he believes, can be used as the basis for fundamental inquiry into the still-shrouded secrets of pathology. Thus by doing steady, small good for the town, he might do some great good for the world. He further intends to combine enlightened treatment of his own patients with efforts to introduce reforms into the conduct of the larger medical profession of the region.

To want all this is to want a great deal, and it is precisely in the determination to live a life that contains, and resolves, so many contradictions that Lydgate's originality lies. The attempt to combine functions—or, in the case of dispensing drugs and holding medical consultations, to keep them separate—was particularly important because of the highly specific and hierarchical way the profession was organized in the first part of the nineteenth century. Physicians were gentlemen who offered diagnostic consultations on internal medical problems to the middle classes and to people "of quality." Surgeons were usually men of less certain social standing who ranged more freely over the class spectrum, performing what we would now call operations. Apothecaries, often medical shopkeepers, played the role of a kind of "people's" doctor who concentrated on dispensing drugs that they themselves compounded. The progress of medical reform, resulting in the Medical Act of 1858, was a matter of combining into the work of one professional the separate functions of physician and surgeon and isolating them from the drug-dispensing role, which was left to druggists and shopkeepers. These "general practitioners," as they were called, first appeared in the 1830s, and their first professional organization, the forerunner of the B.M.A., was incorporated in 1832 in Worcester as the Provincial Medical and Surgical Association. The word "Provincial" is significant here, because it was only outside London, where the Royal College of Physicians, the College of Surgeons, and the Apothecaries Hall enforced a strict separation of the profession, that someone like Lydgate could overcome "the irrational severence between medical and surgical knowledge" (ch. 15, p. 108). These conditions extended to medical education as well. The education received by the fashionable London physicians at Oxford and Cambridge was aimed less at transmitting medical knowledge than at forming gentlemen who would know how to behave when called to attend patients in the great houses of the land. Although Lydgate's birth and manners clearly place him in this social circle, he gives up this path in favor of a less prestigious one that will take him closer to the sources of "effectual" knowledge in his calling. This means London, Edinburgh, and Paris instead of Oxford and Cambridge for training, and the provinces instead of London for practice. These new centers gained their authority by the assertion of a new equation between professional status and, rather than class, professional expertise. The very possibility of a doctor's being an expert—that is to say, the possibility of a connection between his professional activity and the actual curing of people—first became thinkable at this time. Lydgate intended to exploit the current state of knowledge and add to it. Thus, by situating Lydgate at a particular phase of medical reform, George Eliot defines the quality of his originality. He works to rationalize the functions of the medical practitioner, to remove himself from the temptation to yield to the public's clamor for drugs, and to establish his training on a basis of skill and science rather than on birth. Fighting for such measures in the late 1820s meant fighting on a sparsely populated frontier, encouraged only by lone voices like that of Thomas Wakely and *The Lancet* and unsupported by the organized solidarity that came later. Reform, itself the dream of a world susceptible to the direct rationality of the individual mind, became under these lonely circumstances less a movement for institutional change than an assertion of the individuality and originality of the self.[2]

Nowhere is Lydgate's desire to be an originator more evident than in his ambitions as a scientist. He is potentially a "discoverer" who lives at a time "when a bold sailor, even if he were wrecked, might alight on a new kingdom" (ch. 15, p. 109). Although the mention of the fatal contingencies of exploration strikes us as a bit overdramatic in speaking of *scientific* exploration, we are swept away by the image of Lydgate as "a spirited young adventurer" and the state of pathology in 1829 as an undiscovered "fine America." George Eliot is at pains to render vocation usable in the novel by identifying a particular stage in its development.

Lydgate's point of departure is the work of the French biologist M. F. X. Bichat who "first carried out the conception that living bodies, fundamentally considered, are not associations of organs which can be understood by first studying them apart, and then as it were federally; but must be regarded as consisting of certain primary webs of tissues of which various organs — brain, heart, lungs, and so on — are compacted" (ch. 15, p. 110).[3] Bichat, however, did not use a microscope and died at the age of thirty-one. Lydgate, having his life ahead of him and having the advantage of the new tool of exploration, hopes to venture beyond his predecessor's notion of the tissues "as the ultimate facts in the living organism." Might there not, he conjectures, be a more "primitive tissue" which formed "some common basis from which they all started, as your sarsnet, gauze, net and satin and velvet from the raw cocoon?" Lydgate wants to penetrate the multiplicity of structures to find in "the very grain of things" a unitary source. Unfortunately, despite his admirable efforts, Lydgate has not quite put the question "in the way required by the waiting answer," and he is destined to miss the "right word" that would have put him into the line of inquiry which biology was to take up. On the basis of notes in the *Middlemarch Quarry*, W. J. Harvey has pointed out that George Eliot thought of Lydgate as operating at a point just prior to the great advances in cellular theory by the Germans Schleiden and Schwann in the 1830s.[4] The next step was to be from the tissue to the cell, and, at least from George Eliot's vantage point in 1870, the truth of biology had to do with irreducible multiplicity rather than with a unitary source. "The brief and glorious career of Bichat," we are told, "like another Alexander, left a realm large enough for many heirs," and we are clearly meant to see Lydgate as a Ptolemy or a Seleucus who lived in the interregnum before the rise of Rome.

Lydgate's search for a "primitive tissue" puts him squarely among the company of *Middlemarch*; in regard to vocation this is the great homology of the novel: Causaubon and his Key, Will and the "single measure" of reform, Dorothea and her plans, and the narrator and the unitary fabric of community. In a world in which vocation involves the search for an original source, Lydgate's ambition is the most revealing, because he literally seeks the origins of life itself. Unlike Casaubon's avoidance of progressive scholarship in his field, Lydgate devours the latest literature, and it is only because of an irony of timing that he cannot know of the advances—again by Germans—that would have put his own work into the mainstream of discovery. Compared, also, with Will Ladislaw's sense of vocation, Lydgate's is doubly attractive, for as a genius, Will believes that his creative powers derive directly from himself and, moreover, that they have been liberated by his break with the past. Lydgate makes no such claims: he knows he stands on the shoulders of his predecessors and that anything he hopes to accomplish will make sense only in terms of their work.

THE FAMILY OF SCIENCE

Lydgate's relationship to the history of medicine goes beyond a sense of indebtedness. He thinks of the past as an unbroken chain of discovery and transmission, advanced by personal courage in the face of convention and superstition. Despite jumps of hundreds of years, there is a manifest succession of masters and disciples; for Lydgate, Vesalius, Bichat, and Jenner are the spiritual fathers of a new family. An orphan like Dorothea, Celia, Will, and Bulstrode, Lydgate has no inheritance and must make his own way in the world. Because becoming a doctor, in the eyes of his guardians' society, means irrevocably lowering himself, Lydgate forgoes the advantages that privileged birth would have brought him. The fact is that Lydgate cares nothing for the legacies of his family, neither his father's career as a military man nor his guardians' standards of propriety. As a replacement, he attaches himself to a family of an entirely different order: the life of vocation.

In his new substitute family, Lydgate chooses as his "father" the sixteenth-century anatomist Andreas Vesalius (1514-1564).[5] This connection to historical figures — with a sense of either intense identification or spiritual rebirth — touches all the novel's aspiring originators: Will as another Byron or Burke, Casaubon sitting in Rome for his portrait as Aquinas the "heavenly doctor," and dozens of images of Dorothea as St. Theresa, the Virgin Mary, and other redemptive figures. In each case the line between novelistic character and historical figure is inflected differently, leading, by comparison, to qualifications of the character's originality. Versalius was born in Brussels, the son of a well-to-do court apothecary, and was educated at Louvain and afterward at the University of Paris. In Paris he revived the study of empirical, descriptive anatomy of the human body after the discipline had remained in a stylized and academic mold for the twelve hundred years since Galen. Because his new findings clashed with received literary medical traditions and also because of his covert methods of procuring cadavers for dissection — Lydgate frightens Rosamond with this account at the end of chapter 45 — Vesalius left Paris for Padua, where at the age of twenty-three he was appointed professor. Several years later with the help of artists he published his masterpiece, the *De humani corporis fabrica* (Basel, 1543), which, in addition to being one of the magnificent books of the sixteenth century, began the modern study of biology. His creative work finished by the age of twenty-eight, Vesalius left Padua to become physician to Charles V and then to Philip II. At the age of fifty he undertook a pilgrimage to Jerusalem but died on the way back.

There is much here for Lydgate to identify with. Lydgate, too, faces resistance both from popular superstition and from sterile academic circles; he also leaves the established academic centers of his time for places more hospitable to empirical scientific research; he too hopes while he is still young to become the founder of a new phase of biological knowledge. Yet the comparison with Vesalius' life, as viewed by reader and narrator, continues to work along ironic lines. Although both men, having spent themselves early in life, filled out the rest of their days with a comfortable life in society—Vesalius at court and Lydgate between London and the German spas—Lydgate's early career is a complete failure, his "retirement" made in capitulation rather than in triumph. An additional point of disjunction is tied to one of the chief ironies of *Middlemarch* as a whole: the gap between the literary ambitions of the leading characters and the texts they eventually manage to produce. Lydgate lives in the reverie of the ground-breaking researches that will result from the patient application of the microscope to his clinical experience in Middlemarch, but in the end his treatise on gout must stand embarrassingly next to Vesalius' monumental *Fabrica*. Most significant is the diverging directions of their anatomical studies. Vesalius was concerned with how the individual organs make up the *fabric* of the human body, bringing to the task a Renaissance sense of wonder at the perfection of the whole. Lydgate, instead of concentrating on the ends and purposes of life, seeks to penetrate more and more deeply, and less successfully, into its origins.

For Lydgate the search for the origins of life is also a search for personal origins. He chooses the chain of scientific tradition to give him the sense of anteriority and paternity he desires. But Lydgate's "family" offers the possibility of transcending earthly families. By furthering the work of the "great originators" and the "Shining Ones" he proceeds on a "course toward final companionship with the immortals" (ch. 15, p. 109). He does not ultimately arrive, but in a century when the works of the great heroes of science, letters, and industry were read as sacred texts and their lives chronicled and imitated, the attempt to join this glorious company was a serious matter.

If Lydgate had instead chosen to root his life in a real family, he would have had difficulty finding encouraging models in the world of *Middlemarch*. Except for the Garth family, which floats in its own idealized space of economic traditionalism, families are either unsparingly dissected and shown to leave harmful legacies to their offspring (like the Vincys), satirized as narcissistic institutions (Celia and the worship of Baby), or ignored altogether. Lydgate and Rosamond and Will and Dorothea are marriages that produce children (and thus become families) only outside the novel in the "Finale"; and the union of Dorothea and Casaubon must be considered the greatest representation in our literature—excepting perhaps the marriage of Isabel Archer and Gilbert Osmond—of the sterile marriage for which the idea of children, if thinkable at all, remains only a grim joke. In the end Rosamond's miscarriage is the closest we come. Not only do children in their own right (except once again for the Garths) receive no treatment in the novel, but the childhood of the major characters is also unavailable to us. Aside from the brief mention of some schooling in Switzerland, we know nothing about Dorothea or Celia before the moment they speak to us in their own voices on the first page of the novel. Lydgate's vocational prehistory is all that is given us of his early life, and since he is an orphan like the Brooke sisters, there is no question of the effect of family upbringing. Family influence or heredity in *Middlemarch* is nearly entirely absent. Two exceptions exist. Farebrother's family circle can be depicted in affectionate tones, because, containing only his mother, her sister, and his own sister, it is blessed by the absence of the destabilizing forces of sexuality. Bulstrode, whose life as a young man is recounted at the time of his unmasking, remains an orphan whose "true" life begins when he declines his right vocation (the dissenting ministry) for an opportunist "vocation" of disposing of stolen goods.

When Virginia Woolf called *Middlemarch* one of the few novels written specifically for adults, she called attention to one of the distinguishing features of the work: that the people of *Middlemarch* are adults above all else. Their parents are dead or unmentioned; their history as children is unrecorded; and their lives as progenitors of families have not begun. The novel's people exist in the space of isolated adulthood. They are the counterpart, in a sense, of the middle classes, who have to make their way in the world (and in the world of the novel) without inherited resources.

In George Eliot's earlier novels the authority of the family fares considerably better. In *Adam Bede*, the Martin Poysers live three generations in the same house and pass the working of the land from generation to generation. Though they may be as idealized as the Garths, they stand closer to the center of *Adam Bede*. They represent the Loamshire setting which, dislocated for a time by Arthur's and Hetty's indiscretion, eventually returns to its timeless equilibrium. Against the Poysers, the Bede family—the unsavory father, the possessive mother, the otherworldly Seth, and the larger-than-life Adam—stands as an organism barely capable of containing the opposing forces within it. In *The Mill on the Floss* this capacity breaks down altogether. Mrs. Tulliver is unable to think beyond the fate of her linen and silver; Mr. Tulliver, after misdirecting his son's education, leaves him as his only legacy a mission of hatred and self-repression; and Maggie leaves childhood with enormous needs for affection and love that can be met only, and impossibly, by her brother. *The Mill on the Floss* describes the tension between the extremity of need the family generates and should gratify and the inability of the natural, biological family to do so. The death embrace of Tom and Maggie in the flood is a way of ending the novel without having to acknowledge the irreconcilability of the conflict.

The growing consciousness of the impossibility of the biological family defines the shape of much other major fiction of the century. Just as George Eliot's career extends from the Poysers to Daniel Deronda, so Dickens had traversed the space between the massive and joyfully reunited families that end *Nicholas Nickelby* and *Martin Chuzzlewit* to the barren bachelorhood of Pip at the original close of *Great Expectations*. Edward Said has charted the life of the novel according to its capacity to represent "the generative processes of life": conception, birth, marriage, family. Dilating on the terminal points of the novel's career, Said demonstrates how its origins have to do with notions of birth in *Tristram Shandy* and its death with the suicides of *Jude the Obscure* and *The Possessed*.[6] *Middlemarch* belongs in a sense, to the penultimate stage of this progression, a stage in which the natural order of the family is no longer thinkable but in which the *idea* of the family is still alive as a model for human organization and a metaphor for the nonbiological bonds among individuals in a new age of humanity. Biological origination and generativity have been converted into objects of study; Lydgate searches for them under the lens but cannot make them good in his life. Yet the family, taken if only as a model of organization, still offers many attractive features: hierarchy, obedience, reciprocity, unconditional membership and love, historical succession, and the authority of the past. Therefore the idea of the family—the imaginary family whose members need not be related through blood but only through a shared concern for humanity—could be appropriated as an adequate vehicle for the novelist's vision of an idealized community.

In the end, humanity as a family that embraces all human beings overtakes vocation as a family that joins the members of a particular profession. Although the brotherhood of vocation is in eclipse here, its spirit is renewed later in the works of James, Conrad, Wilde, and Joyce, which look to art as the only source of paternity and kinship.

COMMUNITY AND INDEPENDENCE

Because it is not realized in the novel, the idea of vocation as a transhistorical fellowship remains only an idea, a plant growing solely in the medium of Lydgate's desire. It was to have compensated not only for the loss of his family but also for the resistance that would greet his reforms in the provincial towns. One of the more poignant ironies of Lydgate's life is that when the resistance does arise, it comes in a form that so saps his energies that he is unable to produce any discoveries or even research with which to console himself. The story of how Lydgate's dream of a redemptive vocation is accosted and finally disarmed is one of the central dramas of *Middlemarch*. In an early chapter in the novel a brief conversation between Farebrother and Lydgate sets the terms for Lydgate's subsequent entanglements.

Chapter 17 begins with a description of the Farebrother household. The Vicar lives in the midst of female society—his mother, her sister, and his own sister—whose support requires all of his income, leaving him unable to marry. Lydgate is introduced, and a conversation ensues about filial piety and the legacy of values parents leave to children. The talk shifts to the preaching of Mr. Tyke, the Vicar's evangelical competitor for the chaplaincy of the hospital. Farebrother takes his guest out of the drawing room and into the study to admire his exhaustive, carefully arranged collection of the region's insects. Farebrother's remarks about the importance of his hobby to him prod Lydgate to reply that, for his part, his determination to give his all to his vocation will leave little time for hobbies. The Vicar switches to the subject of a common acquaintance, a medical student with whom Lydgate had shared an apartment in his Paris student days. Lydgate remembers him as a man who derided the medical profession, espoused French social theories, and talked of "going to the Backwoods to found a sort of Pythagorean community."[7] The Vicar informs him that now the man is practicing at a German spa and married to a rich patient. When Lydgate says he had tried to show the man the futility of his schemes, the Vicar replies that Lydgate might find his reforming measures as hard to carry out in Middlemarch as a Pythagorean community would be in the

Backwoods. The chapter continues with a passage that reveals a great deal about Lydgate's sense of himself and his differences from Farebrother. Farebrother is speaking.

". . . you are eyeing that glass vase again. Do you want to make an exchange? You shall not have it without a fair barter."

"I have some sea-mice — fine specimens — in spirits. And I will throw in Robert Brown's new thing — 'Microscopic Observations on the Pollen of Plants' — if you don't happen to have it already."

"Why, seeing how you long for the monster, I might ask a higher price. Suppose I ask you to look through my drawers and agree with me about all my new species?" The Vicar, while he talked in this way, alternately moved about with his pipe in his mouth, and returned to hang rather fondly over his drawers. "That would be good discipline, you know, for a young doctor who has to please his patients in Middlemarch. You must learn to be bored, remember. However, you shall have the monster on your own terms."

"Don't you think men overrate the necessity for humouring everybody's nonsense, till they get despised by the very fools they humour?" said Lydgate, moving to Mr Farebrother's side, and looking rather absently at the insects ranged in fine gradation, with names subscribed in exquisite writing. "The shortest way is to make your value felt, so that people must put up with you whether you flatter them or not."

"With all my heart. But then you must be sure of having the value, and you must keep yourself independent. Very few men can do that. Either you slip out of service altogether, and become good for nothing, or you wear the harness and draw a good deal where your yoke-fellows pull you. But do look at these delicate orthoptera!"

Lydgate had after all to give some scrutiny to each drawer, the Vicar laughing at himself, and yet persisting in the exhibition.

"Apropos of what you said about wearing harness,"

Lydgate began, after they had sat down, "I made up my mind some time ago to do with as little of it as possible. That was why I determined not to try anything in London, for a good many years at least. I didn't like what I saw when I was studying there—so much empty bigwiggism, and obstructive trickery. In the country, people have less pretension to knowledge, and are less of companions, but for that reason they affect one's *amour-propre* less: one makes less bad blood, and can follow one's own course more quietly."

"Yes—well—you have got a good start; you are in the right profession, the work you feel yourself most fit for. Some people miss that, and repent too late. But you must not be too sure of keeping your independence."

"You mean of family ties?" said Lydgate, conceiving that these might press rather tightly on Mr Farebrother.

"Not altogether. Of course they make many things more difficult. But a good wife—a good unworldly woman—may really help a man, and keep him more independent. There's a parishioner of mine—a fine fellow, but who would hardly have pulled through as he has done without his wife. Do you know the Garths? I think they were not Peacock's patients."

"No; but there is a Miss Garth at old Featherstone's, at Lowick."

"Their daughter: an excellent girl."

"She is very quiet—I have hardly noticed her."

"She has taken notice of you, though, depend upon it."

"I don't understand," said Lydgate; he could hardly say "Of course."

"Oh, she gauges everybody. I prepared her for confirmation—she is a favourite of mine." Mr Farebrother puffed a few moments in silence, Lydgate not caring to know more about the Garths. At last the Vicar laid down his pipe, stretched out his legs, and turned his bright eyes with a smile towards Lydgate, saying—

"But we Middlemarchers are not so tame as you take

us to be. We have our intrigues and our parties. I am a party man, for example, and Bulstrode is another. If you vote for me you will offend Bulstrode."

"What is there against Bulstrode?" said Lydgate, emphatically.

"I did not say there was anything against him except that. If you vote against him you will make him your enemy."

(Pp. 129-130)

Farebrother ends the chapter by severely criticizing Bulstrode's contempt for the unredeemed portion of mankind. As to Bulstrode's efforts to oust him from the hospital, Farebrother says that if Bulstrode wished to consider him a mischievous fellow, that was his privilege, for "I am not a model clergyman—only a decent makeshift."

In this passage Farebrother is doing all he can to warn Lydgate of the obstacles Middlemarch will place in the way of his professional plans. That the Vicar's subtle and skillful attempts to get the message through to the doctor meet with obtuseness produces a desperate irony which deepens as the Vicar tries yet another opening, and Lydgate again misses the point. The conversation tampers with our conceptions of the two men: Lydgate the cosmopolitan as against Farebrother the plodding, undistinguished churchman. Yet Farebrother emerges here as a savvy politician who, like an experienced sparring partner with an amateur boxer, tries to work over Lydgate for his own good. He adroitly moves Lydgate back and forth between examining his specimens and considering his observations on the political complexities of life in Middlemarch. Whenever Lydgate begins to resist or to miss the point, the Vicar feints back, invents some agreeable banter, and looks carefully for another opening. By adopting methods of persuasion suited to Lydgate, Farebrother tries to communicate to the worldly doctor what Middlemarch is really like. By embodying in his own style of speech the methods Lydgate would have to adopt in order to succeed in the town, Farebrother shows him politics in action, politics being used conscientiously.[8]

Earlier Farebrother had been trying to get Lydgate to pay attention to the carefully arranged rows of mounted insects in his study drawers, but Lydgate's interest is aroused only by an anencephalous monster preserved in a glass vase. Sensing that classifications of natural objects cannot compete for Lydgate's curiosity with an anomalous, wholly original freak of nature (anencephalous means lacking a brain), Farebrother exploits Lydgate's interest in the monster to draw him into an exchange, stressing that the barter must be a fair one. The Vicar is playfully trying to break down Lydgate's autocratic self-seriousness and to establish in his eyes the validity of modes of compromise and exchange. Claiming that as just payment for the monster he could demand that Lydgate look through all his drawers and confirm his classifications of all the new species, Farebrother announces that although he will relent and let Lydgate off the hook, a young doctor in Middlemarch who has to please his patients should learn to be bored.

Lydgate now takes issue, claiming that flattery can easily result in being despised by the fools one flatters. Rather than humoring people, the most direct way to get things done is to use one's talent, to make one's value felt. The Vicar concurs but sets two conditions. A man must first be sure of having the value or else he will be good for nothing, and a man must also keep himself independent or else, clamped in a harness, he will have to draw a good deal in the direction his yoke-fellow pulls him. Before the doctor can respond, Farebrother characteristically shifts ground and invites his guest once again to scrutinize his collection, with particular attention to his "delicate orthoptera." The problem of independence planted in his mind, Lydgate himself returns to it when they sit down to chat, asserting that for the very reasons Farebrother cited he had decided to stay clear of London and to choose a provincial town like Middlemarch for his work. As a student in London he had seen how a man's best energies could be eaten up by the jealousy of competitors whose knowledge was mere trumpery. However, because in the country "people have less pretension to knowledge" and a man of true value is not a common occurrence, one can follow one's own course there more quietly. One has to give up the companionship of colleagues, but in return one is free from serious challenges to one's self-pride.[8]

Perceiving that Lydgate did not quite understand what had been meant by independence, Farebrother retreats for a moment rather than appear too insistent. He compliments Lydgate on having made a good start by choosing a profession he feels suited for, whereas he, Farebrother, has missed his chance and repented too late. When Farebrother re-opens the question of independence, Lydgate misses the point entirely, thinking that Farebrother is speaking from his own experiences with family ties. Farebrother decides to take Lydgate on his own terms and observes that a "good unworldly woman" need not necessarily be a drag on one's independence, the Garths being an example of this. Lydgate does not know the parents but has noticed a quiet girl of that name at old Featherstone's; Farebrother, meaning that Mary has formed some acute judgements of the doctor, notes simply that she has noticed Lydgate; but Lydgate characteristically interprets the remark to mean that Mary admires him, and he feigns modesty by replying ironically, "I don't understand."

Meeting Lydgate's indifference to the Garths, Farebrother allows the conversation to dwindle for a moment before finally abandoning oblique approaches to his message. Middlemarch, the Vicar plainly states, is not the submissive medium Lydgate imagines it to be but rather a highly charged political field rife with parties and intrigues. Even though the division of men into competing groups sometimes lacks all reason, it is nevertheless inescapable, and any course of action, to be successful, must proceed in the knowledge that it will elicit the favor of one sector and the hostility of others. Dismissing the warning, Lydgate replies proudly "I don't know that I need mind about that"; most men might be entangled by such petty squabbles, but since he is inspired by great ideas and by the prospect of great discoveries, it is of little consequence. He has chosen Middlemarch to serve his own larger aims, and if those interests are furthered by Bulstrode's money for a new model hospital, then despite the banker's religion and politics, there can be no harm in making use of him. As in the case of the bottled monster, Lydgate plans to have Bulstrode on his own terms.

Yet Middlemarch will have it otherwise. "Middlemarch," as the narrator tells us at the close of chapter 15, "in fact, counted on swallowing Lydgate and assimilating him very comfortably." In speaking of the problems Lydgate is soon likely to meet, the Vicar raises a series of important questions about the constraints the social world places on originality and vocation. This brief conversation is a rehearsal of the forces that will later obstruct Lydgate's vocational ambitions, and it foreshadows the end of Lydgate's career, a career like that of the doctor who dreams of a Pythagorean community and ends up in a German spa married to a rich patient. The resistance of a traditional community to the clever outsider; professional jealousy and guild-consciousness; the dangers of sexuality and irrational marriage; unwitting dependence on powerful men; indebtedness and financial paralysis—all these are among the ensnarements that make Farebrother fear for Lydgate's independence.

The preoccupation with independence that is so noticeable in this encounter is one of the critical ironies of the novel.[9] Farebrother, the man seemingly so unfree, so weighted down by dependents, so vocationally compro-

mised, is the one who sees clearly what one has to do to remain free, while Lydgate, convinced that he incarnates the
principle of freedom, is incapable of understanding what it
would take to make his project viable. Also, in advising Lydgate, Farebrother is actually realizing his vocation by acting
as a guide or pastor, while Lydgate, whose vocational commitment has nothing "makeshift" about it, is moving farther
and farther away from his. Like a mystagogue, Farebrother
tries to reveal the esoteric meaning of independence to a
man who, clinging to a reductive literalism, refuses to be enlightened. Independence, as Lydgate understands it, means
aloofness and disdain—even exploitation—of others who
would tamper with the solitary generativity of the self; this
path, the Vicar teaches, inevitably allows the despised
others to possess the self and drain it of its independence.
But is it not possible, he asks, that by living a life in community, a life informed by the habits of exchange and compromise, one paradoxically can be most free of dependence
and most capable of creativity? By putting in Farebrother's
mouth the vision of a symbiosis between the aggrandizing,
individualism of vocation and the relentless politics of community, George Eliot discloses a glimpse of the novel she did
not write. Lydgate's life might have been played out in this
way. But Farebrother's teaching is ignored, and from this
point on, we have a story about the irreconcilable conflict
between vocation and the social life.

THE NECESSITY OF CLASSIFICATION

Farebrother's insistence that Lydgate examine his specimens is not a meaningless caprice. That Farebrother is an
aficionado of natural history and Lydgate a professional
student of biology are significant distinctions for understanding the subsequent failure of the doctor's career. Farebrother's concerns originate in the previous century. In its
inquiry into the natural world, the passion of the eighteenth
century was for classification. According to natural histor-

ians like Linnaeus and Bonnet, nature could be understood by grouping its phenomena into sets of differences and similarities, into families and kingdoms, genera and species. To build such immense and complex systems, arranged as hierarchies and chains of being, it was necessary to determine which characteristics—say the arrangement of stamens in plants or the hoofs of mammals—could serve as keys to a consistent and uniform classification. In the late eighteenth century and the beginning of the nineteenth the focus of scientific work passed from taxonomy of this sort to an interest in organic function. Transitional figures like Cuvier, Bichat (chapter 15), and Brown (mentioned above in the bartering for the monster) asked if there might not be functions that are fundamental to all living things. Exploring this line of reasoning with the intensive use of the microscope, biologists described the cell, its nucleus and protoplasm. Rather than identifying a specimen's location in a comprehensive plan, advanced observers were now eager to explore its organic structure. The idea of organicism permeated notions of artistic creation and political theories of community and became an essential element in George Eliot's conception of the epic totality of the novel.[10]

Farebrother is a figure from the sociology of natural history in the eighteenth century. Pursued as an avocation by gentlemen and clergymen (there being no way for a gentleman to base himself professionally in these studies except for such a rare office as the secretary to the Linnaean Society) the study of natural history could be realized by collecting the flora and fauna of one's own region and arguing in the journals over the classification of new species—and all this without setting sail, as Darwin was shortly to do, to exotic islands. Lydgate, on the other hand, is the new man of the new science of biology. Lydgate avers, "I have never had time to give myself much to natural history. I was early bitten with an interest in structure, and it's what lies most directly in my profession. I have no hobbies besides" (ch. 17,

p. 128). Lydgate makes sure to differentiate himself from his friends on these two counts: he is a partisan not of taxonomic classification, but of the "advanced" inquiry into organic structure, and he is a man who brooks no division between his passions and his work. Even if he wields clear authority over the Vicar in these areas — the reader of the 1870s already knew that science would progress in Lydgate's path and that the professions would come into their own after his example — Lydgate displays such absorption in his own work that he does not take the Vicar seriously. The bartering is all on his terms: he is rude to the Vicar, snubbing his work and, when asked to trade, offering a volume that could only be of interest to himself.

With the sense of superiority of the newly enlightened toward the long benighted, Lydgate refuses to acknowledge that there might be even partial truth in the older system of knowledge. To perceive that biology became possible only as a result of the work done previously in natural history is beyond him. Lydgate's dismissal of the enterprise of classification, with its careful determination of boundaries and its straining to comprehend the multiplicity of phenomena within a coherent system, has dire consequences for his life.[11]

George Eliot repeatedly cites Lydgate's failure to apply to the nonvocational sectors of his life the same rigor of observation he applies to his scientific work: "That distinction of mind which belonged to his intellectual ardour, did not penetrate his feeling and judgment about furniture or women" (ch. 15, p. 111). The unfortunate capacity to shower attention on some species and genera of experience at the expense of others is particularly evident in Lydgate's plans to set up house with Rosamond. Although he is not to be suspected of ostentation or vulgarity, he nevertheless sets in motion a style of living that can never be reconciled to the austerity (in Weber's terms, ascetiscism) demanded by the professional regime he intends to establish. George Eliot reflects on the ease with which we may reform some aspects of our lives while leaving others entirely unreconstructed.

> In warming himself at French social theories he had brought away no smell of scorching. We may handle even extreme opinions with impunity while our furniture, our dinner-giving, and preferences for armorial bearings in our own case, link us indissolubly with the established order. And Lydgate's tendency was not toward extreme opinions: he would have liked no barefoot doctrines, being particular about his boots: he was no radical in relation to anything but medical reform and the prosecution of discovery.
>
> (Ch. 36, p. 255)

Lydgate has the capacity, which the narrator suggests we all share, to separate the ideologically vigorous aspects of life from those that are left to the values of the "established order." Lydgate's habit is the failure to determine consciously the correct boundaries and continuities among the disparate dimensions of his life. He is, in other words, an inadequate classifier of the phenomena of experience, and his inadequacy will eventually be his undoing. He fails as a taxonomer of his own life. What does not fit is simply not scrutinized, and he is content to leave it that way.

Lydgate believes that questions that arise beyond the vocational periphery (women, furniture, money, politics) can be answered by the conventional wisdom that ordinary intelligent men, especially gentlemen, possess. Ordinariness is just the point. Whenever fineness of judgment is relaxed, the moral life recedes into a commonness that has no defense against "the influence of transient solicitations" (ch. 15, p. 111). Lydgate is fatally flecked with such "spots of commonness." His real career in the novel, as opposed to the vocational career he envisions, is the story of his progressive subjugation by the very commonness which lies beyond his scrutiny.

The dismissed returns as the demonic, just as the Puritans believed that any idle moment unredeemed by hard work in one's calling was an invitation to the wiles of the devil. Forces that arise outside vocation meet little resistance in a man who believes the loftiness of his calling will protect him from everything. In matters of love and sexuality, Lydgate believes, one can amply be guided "by literature and that traditional wisdom which is handed down in the genial conversation of men" (ch. 16, p. 122). He views Rosamond in this light, and with a fatal taxonomic carelessness he allows that "distinctive womanhood . . . must be classed with flowers and music, that sort of beauty which by its nature was virtuous" (ch. 16, p. 121). He means his courtship of Rosamond to be only a kind of romantic game, until he is constrained by the community to act more honorably. He takes pleasure in the conventions of romantic sentimentality, especially in talk of being smitten and possessed by the beloved. One of the chilling metamorphoses of the novel is the process whereby the playful exaggerations of romantic banter, ignored and unexamined, become the literal truths of marriage. In the masterful chapter 31 Lydgate begins by disavowing thoughts of an early marriage and ends by proposing to Rosamond. "In a half an hour he left the house an engaged man, whose soul was not his own, but the woman's to whom he had bound himself" (ch. 31, p. 223).

Since Rosamond belongs with the flowers, he could not have foreseen the inflexible will that would smother his own; for Lydgate, marriage will involve the loss of his soul and the surrender of the strength to pursue the researches that are so tied to his redemption. The language of these passages is the vocabulary of entanglement and possession: webs, yokes, weights, chains.

In giving us a romantic courtship and a dehumanizing marriage, George Eliot contributes a postscript to the literary career of romantic love in the nineteenth century. The Victorian novelists were the heirs to the Romantic poets, and it was their particular lot to trace the fortunes of the romantic impulse after it was situated in the world of social and economic relations. In the marriage of Lydgate to Rosamond we have an example of what Weber called the irrationality of romantic love, by which he meant the tendency of romantic love to thwart the prosecution of one's calling in the world. Whether on account of class difference, conflicting economic aims, family enmity, or the couple's self-absorbed withdrawal from the world, love and marriage based on passion determine a sphere of experience that works at the expense of vocation. For these same reasons Puritans sought marriages that would be partnerships, not in the amassment of hereditary property, but rather in the pursuit of salvation through calling.[12] Farebrother has this kind of marriage in mind when he cautions Lydgate to seek as a mate only a "good unworldly woman," that is, an ascetic woman who knows how to subordinate her needs to the higher object of vocation. Yet romantic love is but one element in a system of constraints that operates on the professional plans of Lydgate and other characters of the novel. Politics, patronage, indebtedness, rumor, dependence are other factors worth examining.

5

MIDDLEMARCH: INDIRECTION
AND IDENTIFICATION

THE NARRATOR

In perhaps the best single essay on *Middlemarch,* Quentin Anderson argues that George Eliot emerges in the novel as a distinctive, personalized presence who, more than any of the characters, demands our attention and admiration.[1] The analytic passages of the novel, Anderson claims, yield an image of the narrator as Wise Woman whose understanding is so remarkable that it virtually denies her own creations the freedom enjoyed by such fictional predecessors as Don Quixote and Julien Sorel. If we grant Anderson's insistence on a narrative voice whose revealed personality makes it a figure in the life of the novel (as I think we must), then the narrator's conception of her vocation, as much as that of any of her characters, must be examined. The most useful text for this purpose is not one in which the narrator reflects on her own function, but a description of the satisfaction Lydgate intends to enjoy from his. The passage, from chapter 16, maps with a valuable thoroughness the identities and divergences in this regard between Lydgate and the narrator.

Earlier in the chapter Lydgate attended a dinner party at the Vincys' which served as his first introduction both to medical society in Middlemarch and to Rosamond's charms.

He went home and read far into the smallest hour, bringing a much more testing vision of details and relations into this pathological study than he had ever thought necessary to apply to the complexities of love and marriage, these being subjects on which he felt himself amply informed by literature, and that traditional wisdom which is handed down in the genial conversation of men. Whereas Fever had obscure conditions, and gave him that delightful labour of the imagination which is not mere arbitrariness, but the exercise of disciplined power — combining and constructing with the clearest eye for probabilities and the fullest obedience to knowledge; and then, in yet more energetic alliance with impartial nature, standing aloof to invent tests by which to try its own work.

Many men have been praised as vividly imaginative on the strength of their profuseness in indifferent drawing or cheap narration: — reports of very poor talk going on in distant orbs; or portraits of Lucifer coming down on his bad errands as a large ugly man with bat's wings and spurts of phosphorescense; or exaggerations of wantonness that seem to reflect life in a diseased dream. But these kinds of inspiration Lydgate regarded as rather vulgar and vinous compared with the imagination that reveals subtle actions inaccessible by any sort of lens, but tracked in that outer darkness through long pathways of necessary sequence by the inward light which is the last refinement of Energy, capable of bathing even the ethereal atoms in its ideally illuminated space. He for his part had tossed away all cheap inventions where ignorance finds itself able and at ease: he was enamoured of that arduous invention which is the very eye of research, provisionally framing its object and correcting it to more and more exactness of relation; he wanted to pierce the obscurity of those minute processes which prepare human misery and joy, those invisible thoroughfares which are the first lurking-places of anguish, mania, and crime, that delicate poise and transition which determine the growth of happy or unhappy consciousness.

As he threw down his book, stretched his legs towards the embers in the grate, and clasped his hands at the back of his head, in that agreeable after-glow of excitement when thought lapses from examination of specific object into a suffusive sense of its connection with all the rest of our existence — seems, as it were, to throw itself on its back after vigourous swimming and float with the repose of unexhausted strength — Lydgate felt a triumphant delight in his studies, and something like pity for those less lucky men who were not of his profession. (P. 122).

Although it is well known that the goal of much of George Eliot's writing was to create a community of sympathy with her characters, the analytic passages in which she speaks of them are almost always ironic in tone: the humanness we are encouraged to share is possible only because of the cognitive superiority of the narrative intelligence.

The text at hand begins in the ironic mode, probing the discrepancies in the rigor Lydgate uses to judge the various sectors of his experience. However, as the narrator proceeds to describe the quality of imagination applied by Lydgate to his vocation proper, the ironic distance ceases to intervene between the narrator and Lydgate and inserts itself now between Lydgate and all men whose inspirations are of the "vulgar and vinous" sort. Not only has the gap between Lydgate and the narrator been closed, but the exultation evident in the language at the center of the passage (the "inward light" and the "pathways of necessary sequence") indicates that creator and created have momentarily merged. The fusion extends for most of the passage, breaking only at the end where the judgmental tone returns to note Lydgate's sense of superiority to men not blessed by membership in his profession. While the reverie lasts, in writing of her character, the novelist writes of herself.

Lydgate's flaw lies in his failure to bring "a testing vision of details and relations" to bear on anything but his work. Yet no matter how incomplete Lydgate's use of the empirical method of research, the method itself is obviously sound, and its resolute pursuit even noble. Discipline, fidelity to nature, the energetic investigation of origins—Lydgate's situation is poignant precisely because these qualities of mind are so admirable. Someone else in the novel possesses investigative faculties of the same order of distinction yet does not suffer from the same dysfunction. This is, of course, the novelist-narrator, who is capable of comprehending with the same fineness of judgment vocation itself and all the dimensions of experience beyond it—love, marriage, politics, finance. For the narrator, the origins of commonplace experiences must be pursued with the same fascination and exactitude that Lydgate trains on Fever. In her vocation the narrator is called to address nothing less than the totality of experience.

The narrator as the concealed or covert subject of the text becomes evident in the examples chosen to contrast with Lydgate's inspired reverie about his future as a medical researcher. Where we might expect a description of the inferior medical researcher, we are given instead the characteristics of the inferior artist and his "indifferent drawing" and "cheap narrative." As the text becomes transparent, the image on the verso, that of the good artist, becomes visible, superimposed upon the image of the good scientist. If the bad artist relies on stage props, gross effects, and all the meretricious machinery of sensationalism, the good doctor-narrator is enamoured of another kind of inspiration. The expansive sentence that begins "But these kinds of inspiration . . . " meanders through the center of the passage as complexly as the methods of investigation it speaks of. The

"subtle actions" and the "long passageways of necessary sequence" Lydgate pursues echo unmistakably the narrator's
preoccupation with the "small solicitations of circumstance," the "stealthy convergence of human lots" (described elsewhere in the novel), and all the minute processes
of falling in love and falling in debt.

Although the investigation proceeds empirically, "provisionally framing its object and correcting it to more and
more exactness of relation," the processes are so subtle that
they are inaccessible to even the most powerful lens. For in
the end, the truth can be revealed only by a quality of imagination that reaches beyond empirical inquiry to bathe the
object of study in its "inward light." Here again the narrator
is palpably present: although the innumerable laboratory
images that crowd the novel disclose a principled commitment to the empirical method in narration, sympathetic
intelligence is ultimately necessary to penetrate the recesses
of the human heart. The close of the central paragraph goes
beyond a concern with the observer's precise concentration
to a proclamation of the intention to pursue the very sources
of "human misery and joy," "the first lurking-places of anguish, mania, and crime," "that delicate poise and transition which determine the growth of happy or unhappy consciousness." If until now the narrator has been simultaneously speaking of both herself and Lydgate, in this magnificent reverie of vocational desire any pretense of describing
another has been discarded. When it comes to uncovering
the origins of happy and unhappy consciousness, what can
she mean, if not the novel itself? Ultimately, the correspondence between Lydgate and the narrator is qualified. If they
participate in a shared reverie on the future glories of vocation, they share very little in the way of success. The fruits of
Lydgate's life's work will be a treatise on gout. But the narrator has produced the novel itself, whose palpable reality
signifies that the vocational claims of at least one aspirant
have been made good.

Lydgate throws down his book (most likely Louis' new work on the differences between typhus and typhoid) and basks "in that agreeable afterglow of excitement when thought lapses from examination of a specific object into a suffusive sense of its connections with all the rest of our existence." The moment described here tells us much about the authorial interventions Quentin Anderson rightly considers characteristic of the novel. Based on a study of Eliot's exposure to Lewes' scientific experiments of the 1860s, Michael York Mason argues that these interventions are associated with an enlarged view of the witness's participation in an empirical observation, for after documenting the course of the experiment itself, the researcher-witness proceeds in his own voice to interpret the data before him.[2] While this explains many of the reflective passages in *Middlemarch,* it does not do justice to the enormity of the jump from observation to reflection. In the text at hand, for example, turning away from the "arduous invention" of testing and measurement leads to a leap into the free space of speculative rumination. In this expansive zone the narrator is released from the rigorous examination of a specific object, say a character or an event, and is allowed to meditate on its relations "to all the rest of our existence." This is the margin of imaginative play which marks off the witness's act of observation from the writer's inventive transcendence.

DOROTHEA

One of the most intriguing aspects of the textual prehistory of *Middlemarch* is the well-known fact that the novel as we have it is constructed from two stories conceived separately and later interwoven as a single narrative. George Eliot's success in integrating the Dorothea and the Lydgate materials — the subject of the two narratives — is in a large measure due to the structural affinities between their lives as characters. Both are consumed by an ardent desire to make great contributions to the world, both allow themselves to enter disastrous marriages, and both eventually come to see the failure of their projects. The parallelism is all the more significant, because the channels given to Dorothea and Lydgate through which to realize their aspirations are fundamentally different. Although there are serious obstacles in Lydgate's path, he nevertheless has within reach a vocation which, if he could make it good, would be an adequate vehicle for his ambitions. As "certain callings," medicine and science are identifiable and legitimate ways of working in the world, ways in which Lydgate's worth might properly be judged. The same intensity of vocational desire marks Dorothea's existence, the same conviction that the self's value is established by its work in the world, and the same need to originate some great good publicly identified with its originator. Yet as a woman, no effectual calling is available to her. Denied the possibility of vocational expression, she must either resign her aspirations or try as best she can to realize them through the life of her husband and through the modest means open to her as a married woman. Rather than resign, Dorothea marries—and marries again —and so, in terms of the novel, her life becomes a study of the essentially mediated nature of the relationship between women and originality.

This aspect of *Middlemarch,* we are told at the very beginning, will be about proximity and secondariness: since a woman can never fully arrive at the good, her life can occupy a space which is only near the good; from there, nevertheless, she must constantly strive to overcome a condition that by definition cannot be altered. The epigraph to chapter 1 from Beaumont and Fletcher's *The Maid's Tragedy* makes the point.

> Since I can do no good because a woman,
> Reach constantly at something that is near it.

The narrative attitude toward this relation is deeply divided. The body of the novel is the story of how Dorothea's desires must be cleansed of egoism before she is able to do the real good she had always claimed for herself. Yet the "Prelude" and the "Finale," which parenthesize the body of the novel, speak almost exclusively of the intractable social conditions that prevent women's strivings from coming to significant expression. The "Prelude" argues that in the absence of a "coherent social faith," brave women's struggles to respond to a great idea and "to shape their throught and deed in noble agreement" must seem to the common eye "mere inconsistency and formlessness": "Here and there is born a Saint Theresa, foundress of nothing, whose loving heart-beats and sobs after an unattained goodness tremble off and are dispersed among hindrances, instead of centering in some long-recognisable deed." By being denied access to the world, a woman is also denied the power of vocation to "center" moral energies into a single "long-recognisable deed." From indefiniteness and dispersion there is no escape. The "Finale" makes clear that Dorothea has been saved from total indefiniteness by marriage to Will; as the mother of children and as the wife of an "ardent public man," she is able at least to perform the faithful unhistoric acts on which the "growing good of the world is dependent." Yet George Eliot never allows it to be forgotten that the outcome of Dorothea's life is an alternative to the larger life she might have led. Whether the phrase is the more radical "prosaic conditions" of the first edition or the "imperfect social state" of the Cabinet edition, we are returned to the fact of society's role in constraining the expression of Dorothea's ambitious yearnings.

As forethoughts and afterthoughts, the "Prelude" and the "Finale" remind us of an ideological intention that was never wholly assimilated into the imaginative density of the work. As statements which parenthesize the text, the "Prelude" and the "Finale" must yield to the dramatic record of Dorothea's hopes and disappointments in the novel proper. The internal treatment of Dorothea centers less on the limi-

tations of the environment and more on the morally dangerous problems of originality and aspiration. The famous description of Dorothea at the beginning of the novel is much
to the point: "Her mind was theoretic and yearned by its
nature after some lofty conception of the world which might
frankly include the parish of Tipton and her own rule of
conduct there" (ch. 1, p. 6). Dorothea's sensibility is charac-
terized by the same yoking of mind and ardor as was stressed
in the birth of the "intellectual passion" that turned Lydgate
toward medicine. However, whereas Lydgate steels himself
for an active life of service and experimentation, Dorothea's
yearning realizes and spends itself in the realm of lofty ideas
and conceptions. Her "soul hunger" is essentially spiritual-
intellectual, fulfilled by an intensity of conception rather
than by execution. In her reverie she soars to lofty heights
from which she looks down upon her own village, trying
somehow to find room for it in the grandness of her
thoughts. The "rule of conduct" is perhaps the personal discipline which, founded on lofty ideas, would be appropriate
to her behavior in the parochial parish of Tipton. The rule
of conduct, however, may not be for herself alone. Ideas of
monastic discipline circulate in several contexts in the novel.
In the "Prelude," Saint Theresa finds her "epos" in the reform of a religious order, just as her modern counterpart is
destined to be a "foundress of nothing." In Rome Dorothea's
portrait is painted as Santa Clara, the thirteenth-century
noblewoman of Assisi who took vows of poverty and founded
the rule of the Poor Clares (ch. 22, p. 160). The secularized
version of the image appears in chapter 37, where Will
promises not to do or say anything Dorothea would disap-
prove of. "That is very good of you," she replies, "I shall
have a little kingdom then, where I shall give laws. But you
will soon go away, out of my rule" (p. 269). If the rule of
conduct is of this sort, then Dorothea's aspirations are really
to place Tipton under the discipline of a religious order over
which she would preside as the superior authority.

The subtle mixture of benevolence and personal authority is characteristic of the schemes and plans Dorothea originates throughout *Middlemarch*. In the opening pages of the novel she is preoccupied with drawing plans for a series of model laborers' cottages. If the houses of tenant-farmers were decent structures, she believes, their lives would be happy, and they would then be able to return the "duties and affections" their landlords expect of them. When Sir James Chettam expresses interest in building cottages on his estate — there would never be any chance of it on her tight-fisted uncle's land — Dorothea is overcome by a vision of the entire parish building cottages in imitation, thereby making "the life of poverty beautiful!" (ch. 3, p. 23). Sir James soon learns that he has been making a fool of himself, since Dorothea does not take him seriously as a suitor, and Dorothea is soon drawn away from her plans by her marriage to Casaubon. (On her return from the Continent she finds that Sir James has gone ahead with the plans.) When Dorothea becomes mistress of a large estate in her own right, she is secretly disappointed to discover that the poor of Lowick are clean and well taken care of, leaving little room for the play of her solicitude.

Shortly after her husband's death Dorothea declares that a second marriage is out of the question, because she will be completely absorbed in carrying out a new set of plans. This time she is not concerned with anything so modest as a few model cottages; she has in mind an entire colony. "I should like to take a great deal of land, and drain it, and make a little colony, where everybody should work and all the work should be done well. I should know every one of the people and be their friend" (ch. 55, p. 401). As an alternative to marriage and family, and a Faustian one at that, Dorothea will live out the second part of her life in a calling; she will become, in short, a philanthropist. To carry out such an ambitious project, however, requires extraordinary resources, and Dorothea is finally convinced by Sir James and her uncle that hers will not permit anything on so grand a scale. This capital of her own becomes, incidentally, one of the ways George Eliot ties together the parallel stories of Dorothea and Lydgate. Since the money is available and unused, it can be offered to Lydgate for carrying on the work of the hospital and for effecting his liberation from Bulstrode.

Dorothea's thoughts on cottages and colonies and Sir James's experiments with scientific soil cultivation place them squarely in the center of public discussions in the fifty years before the passage of the New Poor Laws of 1834.[3] Perhaps no subject was more widely taken up in pamphlets, homilies, and modest proposals than the question of pauper management. The legislation of 1834 signaled a victory for the political economists: in the centrally directed yet provincially administered system, a new regime of cruelty was intended either to discourage resort to the workhouse or to punish those who had given up the will to work. The opposition that was defeated with the enactment of the new law argued that the poor should be removed from the fluctuations of the free labor market and given conditions of security and independence. Rather than the central state machinery, the local communal institutions of family, church, and squire could alleviate the conditions of the working poor. Some benevolent aristocratic landlords considered the poor on their estates as entitled to help as their "own people" and gave compensation for wages, which raised them to subsistence level—a practice called Speenhamland after the Berkshire village in which it was begun in 1795. Other improving landlords experimented with the "cottage system": granting tenants long leases of land for the purpose of cottage building, with small holdings attached to each, enough for a cow, potatoes, and other crops. The attempt failed, because it largely attracted weavers who had little liking for outdoor work. It is to these experiments that Dorothea's enthusiasm for cottage building at the beginning of the novel belongs.

Some men for whom philanthropy was a serious voca-

tion, like Robert Owen and his followers, indulged in benevolent social planning on a more ambitious scale. They
believed that the cottage system did not go far enough, because it further separated men from one another and reinforced the individualizing tendencies of the larger society.
Self-supporting home colonies, based on the abolition of
private property and the establishment of egalitarian relations, would not only be a setting for alleviating poverty but
also for producing a new man. The family would be transformed in the process, for it was the goal of a community
like New Harmony, Owen wrote in 1825, "to change from
the individual to the social system; from single families with
separate interests to communities of many families with one
interest."[4]

Much about these colonies must have elicited George
Eliot's approval. Given the concentration in *Middlemarch*
on the power of the social medium, she would certainly have
supported the "doctrine of circumstance" that was so offensive to the Evangelicals, that is, the belief that the poor owe
their poverty to the wretched conditions around them rather
than to an inherently depraved tendency toward idleness.
She would also most likely have approved of the idea of the
colonies, because they sought to return a disinherited class
to direct contract with the land. Furthermore, although she
would not have endorsed any practical tampering with the
family, she obviously displays sympathy in the novel with the
desire to overcome the self-absorbed inwardness of the separate family and participate in the larger family of humanity.
Yet if we were to reason that, on the basis of these lines of
sympathy, Dorothea's colonial dreams constitute a step forward for her — approximating, perhaps, the communalizing
mind of the narrator — we would be mistaken. Dorothea's
fantasies of the good are inevitably entangled with fantasies
of the self. Her colony will serve as a vehicle for her own
redemption: she will plan it, populate it, legislate for it, and
bestow her friendship and attention on each of its inhabi-

tants. In regard to this entanglement of private need with public task, Dorothea's notions also closely resemble the projects of the Owenites, who could never quite reconcile their vision of classless egalitarianism with the desire to maintain some paternalistic control over the governance of undertakings they had originated and financed.

Dorothea languishes for the good, but she will have it only on certain terms: as the mother superior of a poor order, as the patronness of an agricultural colony, as the legislator of a petty kingdom. The paternalism in Dorothea is revealed in the distance she envisions between benefactor and recipient. The area in which the good can be done is not where Dorothea finds herself at the moment, within the circle of gentry and professional men of Middlemarch, but rather somewhere far away: down among the poor or re-moved to a colony in the future — a preserve of goodness. Acting across a distance, Dorothea need never be touched by her generosity; she can attain salvation without giving up anything that it really hurts to give up.

The novel requires, of course, that she be disabused of these illusions, and her ordeal is effective precisely because it comes from unexpected quarters. When Dorothea arrives at Lydgate's home in chapter 77 in order to explain the doc-tor's situation to his wife, she accidently witnesses Will's flir-tatious joking with Rosamond and rushes to interpret his behavior as indifference to herself. The incident makes her fully conscious of the intensity of her love for Will, and she struggles through the course of an anguished, sleepless vigil to rise above feelings of jealousy and betrayal to a vision of the interdependent destinies of all men. Although Rosa-mond has toyed with the man on whom Dorothea's happiness depends, Dorothea nevertheless remains true to her respon-sibility to Lydgate and undertakes once again her mission of reconciliation to Rosamond. Dorothea is called to the good at the expense — so it seems at the time — of her own happi-ness, and what is more, the call comes from no exotic distance but from a source uncomfortably close at hand. Dorothea learns that in the community of interdependent souls the moment of self-sacrifice comes at its own time, not in a future of one's choosing. Similarly, the person we help is chosen for us by virtue of proximity only, because he *happens* to be our neighbor.[5] Dorothea's dream had been to transcend her circumscribed social life and reach a plane of memorable action. But the "embroiled medium" cannot be bypassed, and it is *here* that Dorothea's test has come. She would certainly prefer that someone else stand in Rosamond's place, but it happens to be Rosamond, and she has accepted it.

Dorothea seeks dramatized self-sacrifice not only through the quasi-vocational means of good works but also through marriage; and, as she is shriven in one, so she is also in the other. Traditionally considered, marriage was a woman's "calling" in the sense that it offered a "certain" and established life-project directed toward a higher goal. However, in marriage a woman's direct engagement with the world was decidedly mediated by her husband: her fulfillment came from his achievements in the larger culture, from the mothering of his children, and, in the case of a provincial lady, from whatever local acts of benevolence were possible because of his social position. Although George Eliot makes it clear that this is not a true substitute for vocation, she nevertheless acknowledges that the self-effacement necessarily involved in marriage can either be unrealistic and self-serving or dedicated and genuinely helpful.

Dorothea's marriages embody these two possibilities. Marriage to Casaubon promises transcendence of the narrow ignorance of female knowledge, the "inconvenient indefiniteness" to which a woman's passion for great ideas is condemned. "The union," as Dorothea envisions it before the proposal, "would deliver her from girlish subjection to her own ignorance and give her the freedom of voluntary submission to a guide that would take her along the grandest path" (ch. 3, p. 21). To be only an amanuensis to such a man, she believes, would be enough. The extended irony of the actual marriage is, of course, that all the metaphors of secondariness, self-sacrifice, and subjugation come true with a demonic literalness. Through her ordeal, Dorothea discovers the difference between the romantic desire for self-sacrifice and the actual experience of being sacrificed. She receives nothing in return, no access to the larger life she yearns for. Rather than being warmed by proximity to the truth, she becomes a copyist of fictions that counterfeit the origins of the truth.

Yet after the ordeal with Casaubon, Dorothea marries again. George Eliot makes much of Dorothea's initial proclamations against remarriage, indicating that Dorothea's own refusal is related to the strongly stated sentiments of two other characters. For Sir James "there was something repulsive in a woman's second marriage," and in Dorothea's case it would be "a sort of desecration." Will, considering his own future with women, believes that the best is over and, like Frederic Moreau, is ready to retire into emotional widowerhood after having worshiped, but never possessed, his perfect love. Even though Dorothea's marriage was no perfect love, she feels there is something ignoble and sacrilegious about repeating an experience that was supposed to be once and for all time.[6] Yet it is obviously important to the novelist that Dorothea not go into premature retirement as a colonizing philanthropist — and this not only because of the self-delusion of that profession. Remarriage, rather, is a negation of the romantic tenet that what follows a primary, original experience — even if it never lived up to its potential — is a kind of deflated, passive living. It is true, as interpreters of the novel have pointed out, that Will Ladislaw's own romantic unreliability makes him a Victorian "second best," certainly not an adequate counter for Dorothea's worth or a full compensation for her disastrous marriage.[7] Of her second marriage we are told that "Many who knew her thought it a pity that so substantive and rare a creature should be absorbed into the life of another, and be only known in a certain circle as a wife and a mother" ("Finale," p. 611). And in regard to the worldly success of the man into whose life she has allowed her own to be absorbed, we hear in qualified tones of the "young hopefulness of immediate good which has been much checked in our days" ("Finale," p. 611). Dorothea's acceptance of remarriage, in view of all these qualifications, seems to have a double significance. She accepts the fact that, for a woman, direct recourse to vocation is not possible, and that a woman's originality, if it is to be expressed at all, must proceed through the mediation of a man. There are marriages in which the self can be affirmed and gratified — if only obliquely — as well as marriages in which the self is exploited and extinguished, but outside marriage even this little is not possible.

In the "Finale" George Eliot writes that "the growing good of the world is partly dependent on unhistoric acts" (p. 613). Although Dorothea's "full nature . . . made no great name on the earth," her effect on those around her was "incalculably diffuse." These final words of the novel can be interpreted as retroactive instructions about how the work as a whole should be read and how Dorothea's career might be viewed. Life can be valued in two ways: as vocation and as "unhistoric" action. Vocational achievements take their place in the world of culture; they involve the objectification of the self into something that stands on its own in the larger life of man: books, tracts, colonies, discoveries, reforms, improvements, professional services. Unhistoric acts deposit no independent record; they unfold in a personal space beyond which they will never be known: these are acts of kindness, redemption, mothering, and self-restraint.

For a novel so concerned about ambitious vocational achievement, *Middlemarch* ironically records almost no successes of this sort; there are some estate improvements carried out by Caleb Garth and Sir James, the treatises on gout and the cultivation of green crops (by Lydgate and Fred Vincy, respectively), and a book of children's stories (by Mary Garth). Why the novel is an arena for only these minor achievements ultimately involves the question of the genre's epic ambitions. But as a repository for unhistoric —although quite heroic—acts, *Middlemarch* is at times densely packed: Farebrother's forgoing of Mary, Caleb's concern for Fred, and, principally, the stunning moment of Dorothea's return to Rosamond. Although she remains "a foundress of nothing" on one scale of judgment, in redeeming both Lydgate's debt and his marriage Dorothea becomes a savior.

Dorothea's emergence as a savior has been prepared for from the beginning of the novel. On the opening page of the first chapter we are told "that she could wear sleeves not less bare of style than those in which the Blessed Virgin appeared to Italian painters." In Rome Will's artist-friend pictures her as a "perfect young Madonna" or as a "Christian Antigone" (ch. 19, p. 141). She sits for her portrait as Santa Clara (ch. 22, p. 161); in Will's eyes she is his Laura and Beatrice (ch. 37, p. 265); Caleb asserts that her voice is like strains of Handel's *Messiah* (ch. 44, p. 320); Lydgate, thinking of her after she has helped him, declares that "This young creature has a heart large enough for the Virgin Mary" (ch. 76, p. 563); after her all-night vigil she has "the pale cheeks and pink eyelids of a *mater dolorosa*" (ch. 80, p. 578). It has been said that the portrayal of Dorothea at the end of the novel is idealized; this is true, but the idealization fits Dorothea's dramatic function. Dorothea has been described in salvational terms, even when she does not fulfill that role. When Dorothea has relieved Lydgate of his humiliating debt to Bulstrode, and Lydgate speaks of her as the Virgin Mary, she becomes in her actions the redemptive figure she has all along been held to be.

Dorothea's canonization, a kind of moral apotheosis, contrasts pointedly with her image in the "Prelude" as a "foundress of nothing" and in the "Finale" as a wife and mother absorbed in the public life of her husband. Such divergent assessments of character are not limited to Dorothea. It is possible to distinguish within the novel's larger concern with character two distinct lines of valuation. According to the vocational line, an individual is judged on the basis of his contributions to society, culture, and history, in other words, on the basis of works that stand on their own. The other line of value—what might be called the unhistorical or novelistic line—judges an individual by his contribution to the personal moral life of those closest to him (in proximity, not in sentiment), as measured by renunciations of self-interest. Although Dorothea, for instance, succeeds neither in establishing colonies nor in acquiring great learning, she nevertheless functions as a redemptive figure in the "unhistoric" world of the novel. This applies to nearly all of the characters. In terms of vocation, Casaubon is nothing more harmful than a failed scholar; but novelistically, he functions as a vampire which fastens itself to Dorothea's soul and sucks out its life. Similarly, Rosamond, without any vocational aspiration, pursues an active career in the novel as an unmovable counter to Lydgate's ambitious plans. Lydgate's life is cast as a series of professional humiliations, yet by accepting his fate he attains a measure of dignity at the end of the novel.

These two lines of judgment, in their essential configurations of value, roughly correspond to Weber's types of traditional and antitraditional economic ethics. The novelistic standard stresses the older values of family and community and views work as a means of maintaining the physical basis of these institutions. The vocational standard, on the other hand, stresses the improvement of one's own estate, regardless of older ties, and requires that a man be judged on the basis of his worldly achievements. The highly imperfect and unstable integration of these conflicting orientations in *Middlemarch* reflects confusion not only in individual consciousnesses, but in the life of the society as a whole. George Eliot's ideological commitment to a vision of moral community is expressed in the way she requires many of her characters in the end to renounce their personal ambitions in favor of the "unhistorical" family of humanity. But these renunciations, which would seem to constitute a repudiation of the antitraditional ethic, strike us in the end as George Eliot's attempt to impose a desired outcome on social forces which, already brought to life in the novel, are rushing in another direction.

CASAUBON

Dorothea is denied access to the larger world, and Lydgate is made to suffer at the hands of communal opinion. They add internal weakness to their problems, to be sure, but their freedom is to a certain measure checked by external constraints. As a wealthy and respected divine, Casaubon has no such constraints; he possesses both the sanction and the leisure for unimpeded productivity. Yet under these favorable conditions he originates nothing worthwhile and thus he demonstrates that vocational failure can come entirely from within. Casaubon's life's project, the Key to All Mythologies, is an important link in the vocational code of the novel, taking its place alongside Lydgate's primitive tissue, Will's single measure of reform, and a similar enterprise on the part of the narrator. Casaubon's work lies in the pseudoscience of mythography. In the centuries after the Age of Exploration the myths and lore of hundreds of exotic peoples in far-flung colonies poured into Western Europe. Reconciling the myths of ancient Greece to Christianity had been one of the chief intellectual tasks of the Rennaissance, but the arrival on the scene of a welter of conflicting cosmogonies called for new measures. Mythography attempted to impose on the new myths a degree of coherence based on a variety of schemes of systemization. W. J. Harvey, in an essay on the intellectual background of the novel, fully identifies Casaubon's rearguard position in these activities.[8] Not only is Casaubon ignorant of the beginnings of Higher Criticism in Germany—Will taunts Dorothea with this—but he is merely restating positions that were already taken in the eighteenth century. Casaubon is indeed, as Will claims, "crawling a little way after men of the last century—men like Bryant," whose *A New System, or an Analysis of Ancient Myth* (1774-1776) made the case for a single key. By the first quarter of the nineteenth century, in any event, the entire enterprise had been exploded by an accumulating body of linguistic discoveries that closed the door on speculation about the common origins of world civilizations. The pathos of Casaubon's work lies here, in his plodding ahead in ignorance of the discoveries that have invalidated his central thesis.

In the face of the new ethnographic material, Casaubon argues that, if it were interpreted correctly, one could identify within it a common source. Such a reduction could be performed only if the multiplicity of customs and stories were considered corruptions of an original truth: in Casaubon's case, the record of universal man before the Flood and the Tower of Babel. According to this thesis, Greek mysteries, South Sea island creation stories, and African tribal theophanies had all originally derived from the Biblical revelation and were subsequently perverted. Lydgate and Ladislaw, also seekers of a single source, never go as far as this. They manage to redeem themselves by the nobility of their objectives: Lydgate is on the trail of the origins of disease when he ignores the cell and posits the existence of a primitive tissue, and Ladislaw at least wants to make men better when he advocates the single measure of reform. Casaubon's insistence on a unitary source, however, has a different purpose. By manipulating historical records, he seeks to establish the hegemony of Christianity's truth over all other forms of belief. While it is certainly legitimate to *argue* for the superiority of Christianity, Casaubon perpetrates a scientific lie, managing records in order to yield "scholarly" proof.

Whereas the narrator finds much about Lydgate's research that is worth identifying with her own project of narration, she finds in Casaubon's work a complete antithesis. As against Casaubon's falsification of origins, we are meant to acknowledge the narrator's commitment to their disclosure. A commitment to origins does not imply responsibility for presenting childhood and family; these categories, as we have seen, do not figure significantly among the narrator's values. It implies, rather, a commitment to expose the hidden pressures on the social actor that allow the community and the reader to misjudge public actions or to withhold their sympathy. In some instances the pressures are intrapsychic, as in the case of Casaubon, the roots of whose cruelty and paranoia are shown to be a vast and pathetic spiritual emptiness. In Lydgate's case, the pressures stem from public opinion, which knows little of the true horror of his domestic situation and less of the extent of his dependence on Bulstrode. For George Eliot, the integrity of narration involves an allegiance to the integrity of origins. She would have us understand, moreover, that, unlike Casaubon, Lydgate, and Will, *she* does not go too far; she does not try to reduce the multiplicity of separate origins to a single explanation.

In addition to this preoccupation with origins, Casaubon and the novelist also share a vocation as authors. The "central ambition" of Casaubon's life is to make his Key "unimpeachable" from criticism. In fact, most of Casaubon's concern for the fate of his project has little to do with the perfection of his contribution per se and much to do with its reception by others. Making it unimpeachable means making it invulnerable to the depreciations of a Brasenose or a Carp, and for this reason he has stepped back from releasing the entire project for publication, venturing forth only with occasional pamphlets, his "Parerga." His authorship is enveloped in clouds of suspicion and "painful doubts," leaving him in a state of melancholic embitterment, tortured most by the thought that not only may his work be found lacking, but it may never be read at all. He lives constantly in the fear of being found out; his "big mask and speaking trumpet" taken away, he would be exposed as a man with "timorous lips more or less under timorous control" (ch. 29, p. 206). The secularity of his vocation as an author has completely submerged his clerical calling; the two have, in fact, changed places: "even his religious faith wavered with his wavering trust in his own authorship, and the consolations of the Christian hope in immortality seemed to lean on the immortality of the still unwritten Key to All Mythologies" (ch. 29, p. 206). In the "Age after Faith" to which *Middlemarch* undeniably belongs, value and duration are no longer bestowed by God but by the objects produced by human labor. Salvation for Casaubon will lie only in the success of his writings. He has taken his judgment away from God and delivered himself totally to the opinion of this world and its judgments of his work.

In describing Casaubon's anxiety George Eliot is describing the situation of all men whose sense of self-worth is entirely tied to vocational success. The ambitious yearnings of the chief characters of the novel are built over an abyss of fear that appears at moments of disappointment and reversal. As Dorothea asks Will, "What could be sadder than so much ardent labour all in vain?" (ch. 22, p. 165). She is referring specifically to Casaubon and to the possibility that his ignorance of German renders his work useless; but the fear extends to everyone. Despair comes upon a man of immense ambition when he realizes that his past failures and future circumstances mean that the best is over and he will go no further. At the end of chapter 79, Lydgate realizes with horror that this is the point he has reached. The narrator adds that while Will's fate is not yet decided, he too is rapidly approaching the abyss:

it seemed [to Lydgate] as if he were beholding in a magic panorama a future where he himself was sliding into the pleasureless yielding to the small solicitations of circumstance, which is a commoner history of perdition than any single monstrous bargain.

We are on a perilous margin when we begin to look passively at our future selves, and see our own figures led with dull consent into insipid misdoing and shabby achievement. Poor Lydgate was inwardly groaning on that margin, and Will was arriving at it.

(Ch. 79, p. 574)

For the man who creates himself through ambitious work no punishment in the afterlife is necessary, for when he finally accepts the fact that he has stopped moving forward, he is in hell already. When the stakes are so high, the courage to accomplish and to move inevitably involves living with the anxiety of failure and the vision of a future of "insipid misdoing and shabby achievement." In the world of *Middlemarch* this prospect is an occupational liability.

Casaubon and the novelist, we have said, share authorship as their raison d'être. Yet surely there can be no greater contrast with Casaubon's self-consuming paranoia than, as Quentin Anderson has put it, the figure of George Eliot in *Middlemarch*. The narrator as "Wise Woman" spreads her presence throughout the novel, securing our trust with an unquavering voice and a sense of absolute control. There is no doubt that for the duration of the work our ready belief and easy entry into the world of the novel depend largely on our submission to the unequivocal authority of the narrator. To suspect this voice of authorial anxiety would be like questioning the power of the creating God of the first chapter of Genesis. How is it, then, that George Eliot, by far the most ambitious vocational aspirant of the novel, escapes the hovering dread she implies is inseparably part of the act of writing itself?

It has been often noted that among the "originals" for

119

Casaubon — Dr. Brabant and Mark Pattison are leading nominees — George Eliot herself should be included. In the well-known anecdote recounted by F. H. Meyers, George Eliot points to her own heart when asked about the original for Casaubon. In terms of Casaubon's scholarly pedantry, there surely must have been times in the 1840s during her work on the *Chart of Ecclesiastical History* and the translation of Strauss' *Das Leben Jesu* when George Eliot felt mired in pedantic scholarship. The correspondence to Casaubon seems, however, to be tied more directly to George Eliot's mental health during the writing of *Middlemarch* itself. No reader of Eliot's letters can fail to realize that she was one of the great sufferers of literary history. Physical illness and despondency required for their relief the constant application of vast quantities of encouragement and support from Lewes and from others. She was so sensitive to unpleasant criticism, so easily thrown into a series of symptoms, that Lewes had to be extremely selective about the correspondence and journalism that were allowed to reach her.

The attacks were particularly severe during the writing of *Middlemarch*. Aviva Gottlieb has convincingly correlated George Eliot's descriptions of Casaubon's state of mind in the novel with descriptions of her own in her letters.[9] In response to a letter from Harriet Beecher Stowe she writes that her friend's letter "made me almost wish that you could have a momentary glimpse of the discouragement, nay, paralyzing despondency in which many days of my writing life have been past, in order that you might fully understand the good I find in such sympathy as yours — in such an assurance as you give me that my work has been worth doing. But I will not dwell on any mental sickness of mine." In a letter to Alexander Main she writes of "those oft-recurring hours of despondency, which after cramping my activity ever since I began to write, continue still to beset me with, I fear, a malign influence on my writing." Some months later: "my life for the last year having been a sort of nightmare in which I have been scrambling on the slippery bank of a pool, just keeping my head above the water." And to Emanuel Deutsch, supporting him in his own discouragement, she writes: "Hopelessness has been to me, all through my life, but especially in painful years of my youth, the chief source of wasted energy with all the consequent bitterness of regret."[10]

The "creeping paralysis" of Casaubon's inner life occupies the same world of demoralization and despair. What afflicts George Eliot periodically is Casaubon's unrelieved condition: "a morbid consciousness that others did not give him the place which he had demonstrably merited—a perpetual suspicious conjecture that the views entertained of him were not to his advantage" (ch. 42, p. 306). Casaubon suffers from a "melancholy absence of passion" that prevents a man from doing serious work in his calling. When forward motion is arrested, a demonic space opens at the feet of vocational man, rendering him susceptible to jealousy, suspicion, self-doubt, and progressive paralysis.

We see Casaubon, then, through the texts of two writers. One is Marian Evans (or, as she called herself, Mrs. George Henry Lewes), the author of the letters, whose complaints so closely correspond to Casaubon's afflictions. The other is George Eliot, the narrator of *Middlemarch,* whose narrative composure is never for a moment affected by the anxieties of authorship. It would be meaningless to say that one is more "real" than the other—the Suffering Correspondent is as much a self-creation through language as the Wise Narrator; however, it can be said that between these two personae there has been a definite distribution of imaginative energy. Self-doubt and despair have been projected onto the author of the letters, and self-confidence and the aura of wisdom have been introjected into the narrative presence. In pointing to her own heart when asked about the original for Casaubon, George Eliot was hinting at the strange case of her own psychic self-division, strange because it remained unexamined and unanalyzed.

6

MIDDLEMARCH: CHOICE
AND EVASION

The problematic nature of vocational choice is exemplified in the dilemmas of Will Ladislaw and Fred Vincy, who stand at the moment of decision, and in the fate of Mr. Brooke, who all his life has refused to face that moment. Mr Brooke's evasion has caused him to be derelict in his social responsibilities as a landowner; and his case is contrasted with the exemplary responsibility shown by Caleb Garth as a land agent. Although the situation of each of these figures is taken seriously in *Middlemarch,* one cannot help feeling that Will's and Fred's situation would not be quite so desperate, Mr. Brooke's dereliction not quite so contemptible, and Caleb Garth's sense of responsibility not quite so idealized if these dilemmas were not laden with another dimension of value. For George Eliot specialization and choice of vocation are contemporary social realities suffused with older religious ideas concerning a man's one "certain" calling and his responsibility to find it out. The consequences of failure, therefore, involve more than simple unhappiness. Similarly, mismanagement of the land and its inhabitants is not only a question of class responsibility; it also suggests a transgression of man's role as the earthly steward of God's created world. Precisely because Bulstrode claims to speak directly on behalf of these religious notions, his subversion of them makes him the only character in *Middlemarch* for whose sins there is little redemptive sympathy.

WILL LADISLAW AND MR. BROOKE

In Rome Dorothea and Will have the following conversation.

> "And I am quite interested to see what you will do," Dorothea went on cheerfully. "I believe devoutly in a natural difference of vocation. If it were not for that belief, I suppose I should be very narrow—there are so many things, besides painting, that I am quite ignorant of. You would hardly believe how little I have taken in of music and literature, which you know so much of. I wonder what your vocation will turn out to be: perhaps you will be a poet?"
>
> "That depends. To be a poet is to have a soul so quick to feel, that discernment is but a hand playing with finely-ordered variety on the chords of emotion—a soul in which knowledge passes instantaneously into feeling, and feeling flashes back as a new organ of knowledge. One may have that condition by fits only."
>
> "But you leave out the poems," said Dorothea. "I think they are wanted to complete the poet."
>
> (Ch. 22, pp. 165-166)

Dorothea's interest in Will's future is part of a curiosity that characterizes the novel as a whole. In a fictional world populated by orphans who have no direct allegiance to patrimonial property and occupations, men are free to choose their work according to the principle of the "natural difference of vocation." Given the absence of traditional norms, there is no second-guessing their eventual destinations. Who would have thought Fred would turn out to be a farmer, or that Lydgate would be practicing in a German spa, or even that Dorothea would end up by living in London? The hesitations, false starts, and promising beginnings of the young aspirants of *Middlemarch* arouse our curiosity, because they are the first hesitant steps in careers whose outcome no dramatic irony can allow us to foresee. The curiosity about how people make out infects the characters and the narrator as well as the reader. Mrs. Cadwaller's scurrilous gossip is one sort of curiosity, and Dorothea's warm solicitude in this passage is another. Although the narrator usually expresses similar concern for her characters, there are occasions when she assumes a different attitude: the aloof and vicarious pleasures of the gambler who speculates on the lives of others. In weighing Lydgate's chances for success in his vocation, for example, the narrator remarks, "He was at a starting point which makes many a man's career a fine subject for betting" (ch. 15, p. 111). Elsewhere we are told in the same tone that Fate looks on the action of the novel with her dramatis personae in her hand (ch. 11, p. 70).

In this regard, the narrator is conscious of the fact that in appending an epilogue to the novel she is sating an appetite for information about how the characters "turn out." "Who can quit young lives after being long in company with them" she asks, "and not desire to know what befell them in their after-years?" ("Finale," p. 607). In a world where men, rather than being carried by roles embedded in the traditional social structure, must mobilize their energies to *make a career*, questions of success and failure become paramount. Thus the propelling source for the new novel of vocation, the force that for both the reader and the novelist *moves* the novel, is the compulsion to know what will become of people: What they choose to do when they are young, and whether they make good later on.

This is not Dorothea's first inquiry into Will's plans. In the preceding chapter Dorothea breaks into an otherwise conventional discussion on art to ask Will directly, "You mean perhaps to be a painter?: . . . Mr. Casaubon will like to hear that you have chosen a profession" (ch. 21, p. 153). Although Will protests that the life of an artist is too one-sided for him, Dorothea persists in arguing that if he really has a genius for art then he must let that be his guide. In response, Will frankly admits that he could never reconcile himself to being an artist, because he doubts whether he could ever produce work good enough to be considered original.

The passage before us carries over the themes of originality and genius. Dorothea again declares her devout belief in the essentially subjective, individual nature of vocational choice, signifying her liberality by including the arts in her dispensation, surely a sphere of human activity for which she has little sympathetic understanding. The conversation has turned to poetry, and this time she asks Will if he will become a poet. His reply is a tissue of romantic conventions about the soul of the poet: the poetic soul must be an organ of exquisite sensitivity, he goes on, capable of registering every shade of feeling and of turning knowledge into feeling and then instantly turning feeling back into a new kind of knowledge. Since such is the continuous experience of the poet, he does not qualify, for his soul is only intermittently subject to these conditions.

Letting this reverie pass without comment, Dorothea naively points out that Will's rapturous description of the poet's soul has made no mention of the poet's poems. In deflating Will's effusion Dorothea asks the central question about Will's life: can genius exist without something to show for it? Can an identity based on work exist without works? In the iconographic economy of *Middlemarch,* Will is the caricature of genius, or, rather, of the man who is convinced of his genius but does not know through what medium it will be expressed. Given the temporary liberty of Casaubon's patronage, Will proceeds to catalogue the romantic modes of experience, forcing himself into extreme states of feeling induced by alcohol, asceticism, and opium, which are not pleasurable but which seem to be required courses in a proper romantic education. He next passes over into the arts, trying out drawing, poetry, painting, and sculpture in turn. Each potential vocation is eventually abandoned, because "nothing greatly original had resulted" (ch. 9, p. 61). If serious application and drudgery will enable Will only to approach what has already been done in the past, he tells Dorothea in reference to painting, then it is simply not worth doing. George Eliot portrays Will as the reductio ad absurdum of all the ambitious vocational dreams of the novel's other characters. Like Lydgate, he passionately wants to effect an original relationship to the history of human achievement, but unlike the doctor's concentration on a particular field of endeavor, Will takes on the entire universe. Casaubon's "plodding application" and "rows of notebooks" evoke in Will nothing but pity, for he is certain that for genius there are ways of short-cutting tedious perseverance and spontaneously producing great works. While Dorothea restricts her benevolent ambitions to her model colonists, Will is convinced that reform will bring the beginnings of a redemptive process for the whole of England, if not for mankind. For nineteenth-century readers, Will's overconfidence, his impatience, and above all his vocational promiscuity would jeopardize their taking him seriously as a genius. The genius was revered precisely because he had produced extraordinary achievements — the works of a Goethe or a Frederic the Great — and only on that basis was the genius looked to as a guide and a savior.

At some point Will leaves self-indulgence behind to become an earnest young man: he works hard at Mr. Brooke's newspaper, and eventually he becomes a serious, if naive, public man and M.P., "working well in those times when reforms were begun with a young hopefulness of immediate good which has been much checked in our days" ("Finale,"

p. 610). But this does not happen within the novel. Whatever process of conversion Will undergoes—the implication is that his love for Dorothea has made him worthy of her— it is not represented for the reader. But if there is something unsatisfyingly magical about Will's sudden maturation, there is also much that is well done in tracing the constraints and temptations that bedevil his early life.

Will, to begin with, faces the danger of allowing his energies to be dispersed. Expecting his genius to be catalyzed at any moment, he wanders through various activities without seriously applying himself to any of them. Will lives with the unfortunate conviction that, rather than being judged by the outward execution of "particular work," genius, as an inner quality, can suffuse itself into all the possibilities the universe offers. He is at the threshold where, as Erik Erikson has thought of it, a man can advance toward generativity or be deflected into stagnation. From the Puritan point of view, since Will's talents are in danger of being dispersed, his salvation is in question.

Will is also threatened by the specter of dependence. As a man with no hereditary income—he is much sinned against in this respect—and of no distinguished birth, he must either work or be supported. Working would have meant immediately entering a remunerative profession, and thus foregoing a moratorium period to find his calling. But the alternative—being supported—has its own drawbacks: Casaubon's jealousy prompts him to try to exert control over Will's behavior, the issue being Will's remaining in the neighborhood of Middlemarch. Will's proud sense of personal liberty will not tolerate this. His next step is to become an employee-protégé of Mr. Brooke. Their relationship has an air of colleagueship about it, but it turns out to be insidious in its own way. As the editor of the town's liberal newspaper, the *Pioneer,* Will prepares the way for Brooke's candidacy and serves as a mouthpiece for his ideas. This, by itself, is not too serious a compromise, for Will also supports reform, and the newspaper provides a good show-case for his rhetorical talents. The threat comes from Brooke himself. He is very happy to have in Will a man who can take his employer's rambling fragments and spin them into defensible ideas. Brooke, in fact, is very expansive on the merits of the two of them as a "team," seeing in the young Will the roots of a man like himself. In a benignly deprecatory response to Dorothea's plan-making, he comments on the dangers of being carried away by hobbies.

> "Why yes, my dear, it was quite your hobby to draw plans. But it was good to break that off a little. Hobbies are apt to run away with us, you know; it doesn't do to be run away with. We must keep the reins. I have never let myself be run away with; I always pulled up. That is what I tell Ladislaw. He and I are alike, you know: he likes to go into everything. We are working at capital punishment. We shall do a great deal together Ladislaw and I."
>
> (Ch. 39, p. 284)

Mr. Brooke characteristically reduces serious projects to the status of hobbies. The danger inherent in any cause or vocational ambition is its capacity to arouse loyalty and more than casual commitment. He himself has been successful in avoiding any single calling, and thus he has been able "to go into things" in his time without fear of impairing his freedom later to go into still other things. The reason he and Will work so well together, in Mr. Brooke's eyes, is precisely their similarity on this score. Will also "likes to go into everything," and the older gentlemen has seen nothing in Will's behavior to indicate that, in any of the things he has gone into, he would allow himself "to be run away with." Today they are working on capital punishment, and if they go on to remedies for sheep-stealing or rick-burning tomorrow, it will be quite in order.

During his work in Middlemarch, Will has operated, in

Mr. Brooke's words, as the older man's "alter ego" and "right hand" (ch. 51, p. 73). The possibility that menaces Will's future is that he may go further to *become* Mr. Brooke. Mr Brooke is a parody of cheap originality, a caricature of social conscience. He has dabbled in all the social and artistic movements of his day, and now at sixty he is exactly the man Will will become if Will continues to live his life outside the bounds of a certain calling.

Will is at a crossroads, yet it is hard to know what his best choice will be. He could accept Bulstrode's offer of an income, but he senses that Bulstrode's money is ill-gotten even before the full story comes out, and his honor will not permit this. He could ask Dorothea to marry him, but Casaubon's codicil would make it seem that his motives were not entirely pure, and this also would touch his honor. It is important to remember that for a man who considers himself a gentleman but who possesses neither birth nor fortune, honor is the only natural capital he has to work with—lose it and he ceases to be a gentleman, no matter how clever and talented. Lydgate is the novel's example of a man whose honor is destroyed through crushing financial dependency. Living above his means, Lydgate accumulates heavy debts that draw him into a fatally compromising relationship to Bulstrode. Debt is the literal aspect of dependence: a state of bondage in which one has lost the freedom to originate projects. It is the negation of vocation and the negation of honor.

When Will is removed from the editorship of the *Pioneer* by Mr. Brooke after his disastrous experience on the hustings, Brooke declares correctly that in times like these there will be much need for men like Will. The arrival of reform created a demand for a new class of men. Since election to Parliament would now be less dependent on patronage and more a matter of public opinion, men who knew how to shape opinion would be needed, not as candidates themselves, but as part of the "staff" around public men.

Will's power in public speaking and his talent in journalism are skills that will be marketable in postreform times. To follow this course, however, would mean the sacrifice of liberty: Will would be forever containing his own originality and furthering the primary political activity of others. He would always be Lord So-and-So's man.[1]

Will could go to work for himself in one of the free professions where he could remain both independent and a gentleman. In the last resort, Will declares despairingly, he will try law. "I intend to go to town and eat my dinners as a barrister, since, they say, that is preparation for all public business" (ch. 54, p. 395). This option, which seems so natural to modern readers, is raised by both narrator and character with an air of desperation and resignation. The profession itself was unreformed and corrupt.[2] Even if Will becomes a lawyer, his ability to play a primary role in public business will not amount to much in the absence of family and income. Law, like other professions, required a large capital outlay for the period of training and for the many years before it returned enough money to live on comfortably. Without strong family backing, moreover, the chances of a successful political career originating in law were slim.

In his final interview with Dorothea, at the time when her love seems hopelessly beyond reach, Will cries out bitterly: "What is the use of counting on any success of mine? It is a mere tossing whether I shall ever do more than keep myself decently, unless I choose to sell myself as a mere pen and mouthpiece" (ch. 83, p. 594). The pathos here is real; for what Will says is true. The power of the professions in Britain, still in their formative state, extended only to offering a man a modest, if independent, living. The choice is this: selling one's talents to another in order to operate second-hand in significant political circles or living a shabby life with honor.[3]

It is to George Eliot's credit that she unflinchingly rep-

resents the vocational dilemma of the free individual without connections or means. It is less satisfying, however, that
Will is suddenly saved from having to choose. As Dorothea
flings herself into his arms, she sobs: "We could live quite
well on my own fortune — it is too much — seven hundred a
year — I want so little" (ch. 83, p. 594). As she gave Mr.
Farebrother the curacy of Lowick, so she bestows on her lover
the ultimate nineteenth-century kindness: the gift of a living, that is, the gift of capitalization. And magically Will is
redeemed from self-prostitution and mediocrity.

The novel thus returns to the older means of occupational assistance: the patronage system. Dorothea's gift is a
gift of love and a sign of admirable resignation, but it nevertheless redeems Will from the horrors of the open market.

The crudeness and uncertainty of local electioneering
on the eve of reform are raucously evoked in the scene of Mr.
Brooke's maiden appearance on the hustings. The crowd is
not as tolerant as Mr. Brooke's friends of his rambling habit
of speech — here jumping from machine-breaking to Adam
Smith, China, Peru, Dr. Johnson, the Levant, and the Bal-
tic — and a mimicking echo continually throws back his
words. The opposition has raised an effigy of Mr. Brooke
complete with "buff-coloured waistcoat, eye-glass, and neutral physiognomy, painted on rag" (ch. 51, p. 370). The
roars of laughter grow stronger, disjointing his speech more
than usual. Finally Mr. Brooke tries to master the situation:
" 'Buffoonery, tricks, ridicule the test of truth — all that is
very well' — here an unpleasant egg broke on Mr. Brooke's
shoulder, as the echo said, 'All this is very well;' then came a
hail of eggs, chiefly aimed at the image, but occasionally
hitting the original, as if by chance" (ch. 51, p. 371).

This dramatization of the interplay between image and
original has much to do with Mr. Brooke's place in the
novel. Used in this sense, an "original" is the object or person represented by a picture or an image.[4] The missiles of

the crowd are aimed at the effigy, but in the confusion they reach Mr. Brooke himself, as if to indicate that in the press of raw social reality the image cannot for long protect the original.

When he is not electioneering, one of Mr. Brooke's principal occupations is collecting documents about machine-breaking, rick-burning, sheep-stealing, and other evidence of rural violence. His relationship to these widespread signs of opposition to industrialization is that of an aloof documentary photographer to social phenomena: he collects images of the originals at a distance from the actual ground of their occurrence. However, instead of using his documents to record abuses and to provoke concern, they are allowed to accumulate without order or arrangement. In the opening pages of the novel there is a brief discussion about systems of classification that recalls Mr. Farebrother's taxonomic activities. Mr. Brooke asks Casaubon:

> "But now, how do you arrange your documents?"
> "In pigeon-holes, partly," said Mr Casaubon, with a rather startled air of effort.
> "Ah, pigeon-holes will not do. I have tried pigeon-holes, but everything gets mixed up in pigeon-holes. I never know whether a paper is in A or Z."
> "I wish you would let me sort your papers for you, uncle." said Dorothea, "I would letter them all, and then make a list of subjects under each letter." . . .
> "No no," said Mr Brooke, shaking his head; "I cannot let young ladies meddle with my documents. Young ladies are too flighty."
>
> (Ch. 2, p. 14)

Here at the beginning of the novel, Mr. Brooke's rambling distraction is a piece of good fun; we know that Dorothea's scheme for rationalizing the collection of his documents is inimical to what Mr. Brooke's enterprise is all about. But as the novel progresses we realize that the absence of organization is a dereliction of a serious order. Classifying the documents would mean allowing some patterns of explanation to emerge. The social phenomena in question would begin to speak through the documents, giving voice to fear and desperation over the coming of machines and eviction from the land. Mr. Brooke's collection of the documents but his refusal to classify them is not therefore a nonpolitical act; by denying the originals their right to speak he is effectively pacifying their outcry. And thus, by default, his refraining from action is a very political act indeed, for it has real consequences.

In chapter 56 we are given a first-hand glimpse of the problems about which Mr. Brooke collects material. The farm workers of Lowick, having heard that a party of surveyors from the railroad are in the neighborhood, have stirred themselves to a pitch of active hostility. To them the railroad, just then beginning to plan routes and purchase rights-of-way, is a plot hatched by London to cut up the fine land of the parish into "sixes and sevens," and they resent the incursion of these agents into their part of the world. During the haying season when they are all in the fields, they come across the surveyors and are about to rush them with pitchforks in hand, when Fred Vincy and Caleb Garth, who happen to be in the vicinity, break up the disturbance. Caleb tells the farm workers that the railroadmen have no sinister intentions; what's more, the railroad will come whether anyone likes it or not, and the parish might as well make what profit it can from that. Old Timothy Cooper complains that he's lived through several kings and all he's done is watch the big men in London get richer; now with the railroad it will be the same—the poor man will get left farther behind. Caleb listens patiently and exacts a promise of good behavior.

When we meet Mr. Brooke's improverished tenant Dagley in chapter 39, we cannot help sensing an overflow of life which Mr. Brooke, through his procedure of documentary pacification, has not managed to contain. The assault of the Lowick men on the surveyors might be called a rebellion of the "originals," an insistence on speaking for themselves and a refusal to allow condescending gentlemen to manipulate their images.

The revolt of the Lowick men and Mr. Brooke's electioneering are among the few instances in *Middlemarch* in which historical forces are not integrally woven into the private lives of the principal characters. Otherwise, history is presented, as Jerome Beaty has said, through indirection.[5] The chronology of the novel is closely coordinated with the major political events of the period, such as the Catholic Emancipation and the fortunes of the first Reform Bill. The cogs of the two chronologies are so tightly enmeshed that we are prevented from reading the private, novelistic events of *Middlemarch* as being in any sense wholly private.[6] We see how the passions for reform and philanthropy originate within the needs and compulsions of Dorothea or Lydgate, and at the same time we are shown how public forms and cultural optimism create the ground of possibility for what we would otherwise think of as purely private events.

Much of the novel's meaning depends on the stance of looking back: looking back from the time of the writing in the early 1870s forty-five years to the beginning of a culture that had become so complex that its origins had been lost sight of. Written after the first shocks of religious doubt, in the aftermath of the second Reform Bill of 1867, at a time when the "hopefulness of immediate good" had been "much checked," the novel reconstructs the earlier period in the hope of clarifying the present historical dilemma. In Lydgate's work we see the roots of the great sanitation reforms that changed the life of the cities; in his political problems we see the rise of the professions and the establishment of new means of success; and in his research the basis for the great scientific controversies that shook the Victorian world. We see in Will's reforming the second Reform Bill, in his association with the Nazarene painters in Rome the later flowering of the Pre-Raphaelites; in Casaubon's mythography the arrival of Higher Criticism and the giving way to religious doubt; in Bulstrode's and Mr. Tyke's evangelicism the breakdown of High Church hegemony; in Caleb Garth's commitment to "business" the replacement of labor value by money value. For George Eliot, the earlier period was a "time of origins" whose genetic significance made possible the project of understanding that constitutes *Middlemarch*.[7]

CALEB GARTH

Caleb Garth could be said to be the least interesting character in *Middlemarch*. When it comes to a figure so close to her own father, George Eliot's critical gaze had a blind spot. Named for the biblical character who with Joshua returned from the Promised Land to tell the truth, Caleb utters his truths in a cheerful, consistently banal way; his lack of complexity and contradiction make him a fading canvas in a gallery of arresting portraits. Yet this very exemption from scrutiny indicates that, although Caleb might be unessential to the dramatic economy of the novel, to its iconography he has a central relation. Against the vocational irresponsibility and selfishness of the other inhabitants of Middlemarch, Caleb plays the role of the selfless steward perfectly realized in his calling.

In more worldly terms Caleb is an independent estate agent.[8] He is consulted by large landowners on the management and disposition of their estates and is contracted to carry out improvements. When he comes across the farm hands and the railroadmen, for example, he is on his way to assess the worth of an outlying piece of Dorothea's estate in preparation for its sale to the railroad. It is also to Caleb that Mr. Brooke entrusts the repairs on his tenant farms after he has been satirized as a poor landlord in the local Tory press. Caleb knows land, building, mining, surveying, drainage, crop rotation—in short, all the ways to bring out the best yield from the physical environment and to turn barrenness into productivity.

"Caleb Garth often shook his head in meditation on the value, the indispensable might of the myriad-headed labour by which the social body is fed, clothed, and housed" (ch. 24, p. 185). Meditation is not a casual stance for Caleb; labor is his poetry, philosophy, and religion. As a boy his imagination was captured by the glory of good work being done. In describing this fascination George Eliot breaks into a veritable hymn to the workers, which recalls the description of the Poyser's dairy in *Adam Bede:* "The echoes of the great hammer where roof or keel were a-making, the signal-shouts of the workmen, the roar of the furnace, the thunder and plash of the engine, were a sublime music to him; the felling and lading of timber . . . the crane at work on the wharf, the piled-up produce in warehouses" (ch. 24, p. 185). It is as if Thomas Wolfe had been hired by the WPA Writers Project and suddenly set loose in the novel.

For Caleb all of this activity is covered by the word "business," and, according to the narrator, "it would be difficult to convey to those who never heard him utter the word 'business,' the particular tone of fervid veneration, of religious regard, in which he wrapped it, as a consecrated symbol is wrapped in its gold-fringed linen" (p. 185). Business can elicit religious awe for Caleb, because it is uncontaminated by money. "He gave himself up entirely to the many kinds of work which he could do without handling capital" (p. 185). Capital is undesirable not because it is dirty—Caleb is forever rolling up his sleeves and getting his hands dirty—but because it drives an unnatural wedge between man and the material he seeks to shape. Caleb is an idealized figure precisely because he works under the prelapsarian conditions of harmony between man and the world. The Sin in the Garden had brought down on man the curse of unfulfillment; no longer would the land submit to man's exertions. For the other inhabitants of the novel the curse has held sway; their efforts to wrest achievement from the world are firmly resisted by the "embroiled medium" of society.

George Eliot puts "business" in quotation marks, because her use of the word is a conscious transvaluation of its meaning. Caleb's work exemplifies the kind of transactions a man should have with the world: direct, selfless, moneyless. "Business," as it came to be used in the nineteenth century, described the commercial activity of merchants who bought and sold commodities through the medium of money for the purposes of profit in money. This is what Vincy the silk manufacturer does, and also Bulstrode the banker and financier, and a host of "odious tradesmen" and "yard-measuring merchants." The novelist often plays with the artificial boundaries between the term "business" and genteel society. Lydgate's fatal disjunction of vocation and life is mirrored in his insulating of Rosamond from the exigencies of his work life. Accumulating debts and professional jealousies are among the annoyances of "outdoor" business, which he feels should be left at the doorstep before one enters the homely preserve of feminine tenderness. When Lydgate is finally forced to take steps to ease his debts that require Rosamond's knowledge and cooperation, he says, "I have some serious business to speak to you about" (ch. 58, p. 432). But it is too late. He later meets the icy resistance of her will when she effectively undoes Lydgate's efforts to economize by moving into a less expensive home. When Rosamond, the daughter of a manufacturer, goes to Mr. Bothrop Trumbull's office to cancel her husband's arrangement, the narrator wryly observes, "It was the first time in her life that Rosamond had thought of doing anything in the form of business, but she felt equal to the occasion" (ch. 64, p. 478).

In his pursuit of business, Caleb wants direct contact with the material world and resents the complicating insidiousness of money. He would prefer to work only for the pleasure of work, and his wife Susan, herself a paragon of *domestic* economy, has to remind him that work is connected to livelihood. The obvious parallel to Caleb's desire to purge capital from labor is the labor notes that Owenites tried to establish as a moneyless medium of exchange in the 1840s.[9] Labor notes were certificates of exchange based on the amount of labor time invested by the worker, rather than the market value of the commodities produced. Every individual, it was argued, had the right to possess or enjoy the undivided fruits of his own labor — its "full value" — rather than the fractional value left after the entrepreneur took his share and the fluctuations of the market took their toll. Like Caleb, the Owenites demanded that human labor, not money, be made the standard of economic value.

While it is undoubtedly true that by this the Owenites sought to affirm several important questions of principle, one can also imagine that they were moved by troubling questions of livelihood. The full value they sought in return for their labor consisted of goods, commodities, and food stuffs. For Caleb Garth, however, work is its own payment. Struck by the neatness of a scheme to make bricks from the clay of one part of an estate to carry out repairs on another, he exclaims: " 'It's a fine bit of work, Susan! A man without a family would be glad to do it for nothing.' 'Mind you don't though,' said his wife, lifting her fingers . . . 'No, no; but it's a fine thing to come to a man when he's seen into the nature of business: to have a chance of getting a bit of the country into good fettle' " (ch. 40, p. 295). Work is pleasure, and Caleb *is* his work.

Such an idealization helps to locate the other characters of the novel, and the substance of the idealization is echoed elsewhere in the literature of the period. In the *Grundrisse* Marx argues that in the eyes of Adam Smith and the political economists the natural, ideal state of man is leisure.[10] Labor, according to them, is a coerced activity exacted at a price from spontaneous and free activity. Turning the proposition around, Marx, like Hegel before him, claimed instead that labor realized human spontaneity and that what makes it coercive is not its nature per se but the historical conditions under which it is performed. "A society that will abolish alienation," Avineri writes, "will not abolish labor, but its alienating conditions."[11] If labor were allowed to realize human freedom rather than enchain it, then labor could become not merely a means of purchasing existence but its very contents. The figure of Caleb Garth is located at the intersection of such a vision of work in the future and a vision of the independent yeoman of the past.

Caleb, in the end, incarnates a still older figure: the faithful steward. In the Calvinist doctrine of the calling, man is called upon to improve the state of the world for purposes other than his own aggrandizement. He is an agent of God who works unceasingly for His greater glory. Caleb, after this model, lives a life of perpetual trusteeship, caring for the land and increasing its fecundity with no throught to his own material benefit. Does he do this for his own satisfaction? For the sake of the generations to come? For the sake of some higher power? The master and beneficiaries are not clear; we see clearly only the stance of "caring for." This is the same responsibility that burdens Dorothea when she agonizes over how best to spend the fortune from her husband's estate. In this attitude the older, traditional economic ethic is presented in a form transmuted by nostalgia. Caleb does not wish to distinguish himself through original achievements; he takes what is barely enough for himself and, beyond that, improves and enhances what he has touched. His contribution is utterly local; no scheme for scientific crop management will live after him — although Fred's "Cultivation of Green Crops and the Economy of Cattle Feeding" will be praised at agricultural meetings — and certainly no medical discoveries or utopian colonies. In his fulfillment of the ideal of stewardship, Caleb exemplifies, like Dorothea's redemptive acts, the "unhistoric" side of vocation, and as such, stands as a judgment of the other workers of *Middlemarch*.

FRED VINCY AND BULSTRODE

Along with Will Ladislaw, Fred Vincy is the novel's portrayal of a young man in the toils of choosing a vocation. Fred's confusion is perhaps more poignant than Will's, because it can be completely enclosed within the fictional world of the novel. Fred is homemade, and we know him and the range of possibilities open to him because we know and understand the town of Middlemarch. He is not a self-described genius like Will, whose life, moving between the bohemian romanticism of the Continent and the reform politics of London, darts in and out of our provincial field of vision. Fred's life runs along the traditional, "local" track of the novel; his hopes do not participate in the new burst of ambitious world-changing that marks many of his neighbors.

Mr. Vincy would like his son to become a clergyman, a future not at all to Fred's liking. As a landless manufacturer whose fortune is vulnerable to the fluctuations of trade, Mr. Vincy realizes that since he will not be able to give Fred an income, the lad will have to fend for himself. Thus Fred is in the classical position of the younger son who must choose one of the professions for his livelihood.[12] The military is unlikely, because it requires aristocratic connections and a large initial outlay to purchase a suitable commission; the civil and colonial services were at this time as yet unreformed and required similar connections, and, besides, would carry Fred far from the home soil where his life makes sense; law, medicine, and engineering, although becoming fit for a gentleman, carry the significant disadvantage of being based largely on talent and expertise: to succeed, even with prestigious backing, a man has to master a complex body of techniques. The clergy, however, is a different case. Although advancement is certainly dependent on patronage, the connections required are often local; Mr. Farebrother, for example, receives the living of Lowick not from a nobleman or from London but from a local member of the gentry, Dorothea. Above all, the qualifications for being a clergyman are those which most gentlemen already possess. One must have been to university and thus have some knowledge of Greek and Latin; one must assent to the Thirty-Nine Articles of the Westminster Confession; and one must be a Christian gentleman willing to teach the doctrines of the church and represent its interests. Mr. Vincy well knows that, in addition to the fact that the clergy demands no great mobilization of energies, it also no longer demands a deep sense of calling. That a religious professional should also be a religious charismatic is a phenomenon reserved at this time for some dissenting ministers and evangelical preachers like Mr. Tyke, the Oxford movement still being some years ahead.[13] Dinah Morris, the Methodist preacher who fervently addressed open-air crowds in *Adam Bede,* is a woman for whom the idea of vocation is no mere metaphor for inner prompting: she feels she is called by God to convert souls and teach the lessons of the faith. But aside from Dinah, none of the clergymen throughout the body of George Eliot's works have preserved contact with the literal, revelatory base of vocation. In *Scenes of Clerical Life,* the point of departure for George Eliot's writing career, the secularization of the clergy is so taken for granted that their sorrows and struggles as men, rather than as religious professionals, could now be considered appropriate material for fictional study. Thus, in asking Fred to enter the ministry, Mr. Vincy is not asking him to undertake a profession that, in the eyes of the world, demands either passionate commitment or fervent belief. When Mr. Farebrother asks Fred whether he has any doctrinal difficulties that would act as a bar to his entering the ministry, Fred replies: "No, I suppose the Articles are right, I am not prepared with any arguments to disprove them, and much better, cleverer fellows than I go in for them entirely. I think it would be rather ridiculous in me to urge scruples of that sort, as if I were a judge" (ch. 52, p. 376).

In the "Age after Faith" in which *Middlemarch* unfolds, becoming a clergyman is no longer a possibility. It is the one thing Fred cannot go into and hope to keep Mary's love. Yet the passing of this possibility is not registered without a sober sense of the responsibility its demise entails. The ministry once represented the literal, unpsychologized experience of being called; the unavailability of that experience now raises a serious question: what else is worth doing?

If Fred's situation asks this question, his own desires do not go very far toward a helpful answer. For his part, Fred would like to do nothing; that is, he would like to join the landed gentry, not in a big way but enough to allow him to keep some fine horses, hunt and have the means to be a generous, good fellow. This vision of idleness would be offensive if it came from a genuine squire's son, but coming from the son of a textile manufacturer it is ridiculous. Money from trade cannot be depended on like residual income from land, since what one day might be given to sons cannot be insulated from the contingencies of the market. Yet Fred's motivation differs from the pretensions of wealthy captains of industry who sought to buy country estates in order to cleanse their families of the stigma of trade; he wants simply to enjoy life. To the Victorian prophets of work this was an idleness more insidious than that of the poor, for in rejecting vocation a man also rejected the traditional responsibilities of land. Declining to do anything at all was the most despised denial of vocation.

Fred, however, is not without expectations of soon having the means to live as he wishes. He has reason to believe that old Mr. Featherstone will leave him his estate, and his evasion of his father's pressure to enter the ministry is based on the imminent death of this supposed benefactor. Fred thus believes that his identity and place in the world will not have to be invented or achieved by his own efforts but rather will be given him in the future through the agency of inheritance. In this stance Fred takes his place with dozens of other young men in the fiction of the century, men like Pip in *Great Expectations* or Richard Carstone in *Bleak House*. Richard, for example, is a ward of Chancery in connection with the endless suit of Jarndyce vs. Jarndyce. Since the suit involves the fate of a large inheritance, Richard succumbs to the temptation of living in the expectation of inherited wealth. Devitalization, madness, and death result from his dependence on the suit. Symptomatic of his demoralization is his inability to commit himself to a vocation. He makes the rounds of the professions—law, medicine, the army (not the ministry)—but cannot organize his fitful spurts of enthusiasm into a meaningful vocational choice, remarking on each one—in words anticipatory of Fred's attitude toward the ministry—"It'll do as well as anything else.[14] In fact, the chapters taking up old Featherstone's last illness and the grotesques that crowd his deathbed are often Dickensian in tone. One is reminded of the deathbed scenes in *Martin Chuzzlewit* and the ordeal Martin Jr. is put through to become worthy of his inheritance.

For George Eliot, trading in expectations is a variety of gambling. Early in the novel Mr. Featherstone accuses Fred of raising money on the strength of his prospects of inheritance. Although Fred vigorously denies the charge, the old man makes him seek through his father a letter of good character from Mr. Bulstrode. Even if Fred is technically innocent, in a larger sense he is certainly guilty of gambling for time to avoid making his own future. George Eliot's virulent antipathy to gambling has often been noticed: Dunstan Cass in *Silas Marner,* the stunning picture of Gwendolen Harleth in the opening chapter of *Daniel Deronda,* Mr. Farebrother forced to play whist for spare shillings, a desperate Lydgate humiliating himself in the billiards room of the Green Dragon. Fred's dilemma reveals why gambling evokes so insistent a response from the novelist. Instead of making his own future through commitment to some meaningful work, Fred will waste himself in expectation of never having to bother. This aversion to gambling also suggests how deeply commited George Eliot was to the modern capitalist mode of rational risk-taking, as opposed to the precapitalist mode of gambling.

It all comes to nothing in any case; Mr. Featherstone dies leaving nothing to Fred. For a moment it all might have been different, for just before his death the old man wanted to change his will in favor of Fred, only to be checked by Mary, who, in the absence of witnesses, refused to compromise her honor by making the requested changes. As a consequence, Fred must put all his expectations behind him and face a long-avoided choice of vocation. Here also Mary affects his life in a significant way. If Fred wants to be accepted as a suitor, he must choose some work other than the ministry; yet the ministry is the only profession acceptable to his father. In hedging in Fred's life with irreconcilable choices, the novelist is clearly formulating critical questions of precedence and priority. First, Mary makes love conditional to commitment to proper work. As Mr. Farebrother gravely warns: "Men outlive their love, but they don't outlive the consequences of their [vocational] recklessness" (ch. 52, p. 377). In an astonishing displacement of the doctrine of elective affinities from romantic love to occupational choice, Mr. Farebrother declares that if a man is denied love from one woman he can eventually obtain it from another, but not so with vocation: there is a fit, a suitability, a properness which, once botched, can never be made good. Moreover, a man living outside his proper calling is not fully realized as a man and therefore, at least in Mary's eyes, is not worth having as a husband.

Second, the subjective fit of vocation to the man overrides the claims of family loyalty. To choose correctly Fred has to choose against the father. Vocation, as we have seen in the case of Lydgate, is the new family. With Fred this becomes plain in his affirmation of Caleb Garth as simultaneously a new father and a new employer. Fred's rejection of his father is given additional force by the unacceptable nature of Mr. Vincy's work. As a silk manufacturer he imports silk, distributes it as piecework among the weavers of Middlemarch, dyes the cloth, and sells it. Mr. Vincy's work is exploitative in two ways: he "bleeds the poor weavers of Middlemarch dry" with his piecework method of payment, and he cheats the consumer by using cheap dyes that rot the fabric (ch. 61, p. 452). Like capital, Mr. Vincy performs the pernicious functions of a mediator between worker and material and between material and consumer. Within the symbolic code of the novel Fred's final removal to Stone Court Farm and to a life on the land is a refusal of vocation as exploitive mediation and an affirmation of direct relations between worker and world.

Bulstrode is the only character in *Middlemarch* who, in his ideology and commercial activity, approaches Weber's ideal type. Bulstrode is a banker, financier, and philanthropist who views his continued success in business as a providential sign of election and as a prod to use his worldly resources for the improvement — voluntary or involuntary — of the souls of other Christians.

An orphan like almost everyone else in the novel, as a young man Bulstrode feels genuine promptings towards a vocation. As a banker's clerk and a member of a Calvinistic dessenting church in London, he feels himself called upon to preach with his fluent voice on religious platforms and in private homes. "Again he felt himself thinking of the ministry as possibly his vocation, and inclined toward missionary labour" (ch. 61, p. 540). (Bulstrode is, ironically, the only character in the novel who actually seems suited to be called to the ministry.) He does not follow this course, but instead allows himself to become the confidential accountant of a wealthy fellow-congregant who receives stolen goods and disposes of them through the front of a fashionable pawn-brokerage. When his employer dies, he marries the widow and conceals the existence of an estranged married daughter so that the full inheritance might be in his control. After his wife dies, he begins gradually to withdraw his capital from the business and to relocate in Middlemarch. He performs all the operations necessary to establish himself in a provincial town: he marries a woman from the good local stock of the Vincys; he leaves the dissenting chapel and becomes Church of England; he becomes a benefactor of local charity institutions; and he sets himself up as a respectable banker who finances much of the town's trade.

Although resented for his sanctimonious evangelicism, Bulstrode successfully manages his resettlement in Middlemarch, living undisturbed until a man named Raffles enters his life. After Raffles makes it evident that he has a clear memory of Bulstrode's early business activities in London as well as the concealed existence of his first wife's daughter, Bulstrode pays him off and extorts a promise never to return to the neighborhood. Before long, of course, Raffles reappears in Middlemarch, this time with an acute case of delirium tremens; Bulstrode quickly puts him to bed at Stone Court (which he has recently acquired) in order to keep him from revealing secrets to the townspeople and calls Lydgate to attend to him. Lydgate stresses that the patient may be given no liquor when he calls for it, but Bulstrode deliberately does not transmit the instructions to his housekeeper, who, taking mercy on the pitiful old man when he cries for a little something to revive him, gives him a drink, which has the opposite effect. In the meantime the town is buzzing with the scraps of information about Bulstrode's past that Raffles had let out before he was taken to Stone Court. The rumor passes from the Green Dragon to Dunlop's and finally to a meeting of the town council, from which Bulstrode, exposed and derided, is summarily excluded.

As writing, the story of Bulstrode's fall stands out from the rest of the narrative in two ways. Raffles, to begin with, is depicted as one of those Dickensian characters (like Montague Tigg or Quilp) who has no traits other than a malevolent will. Elsewhere in the novel, evil is humanized by explanations of the inner deprivation out of which it arises, but here we have an interloper from London who apparently merits none of the narrator's usually abundant empathy. Secondly, Bulstrode's story is the only element of the narrative that entails extensive exploration of the past; otherwise, nothing is hidden from us; there is nothing mysterious or covert about which the unfolding of present events does not yield adequate information. Such openness was an essential tenet of George Eliot's program for fiction, a program that proposed to locate the origins and motives of human action not in the shadowy machinations of the past, but in the hidden places of the heart. Bulstrode's narrative, however, with its stories of concealed paternity, estranged daughters, illicit partnerships, and altered identities, introduces the machinery of high melodrama into a novel from which, on the whole, it is conspicuously absent.[15]

As one among a number of possible explanations, I would like to suggest that the elaboration of Bulstrode's secret past serves as an imaginative correlative to his own actions. Bulstrode's life presents itself as an utter inversion of the vocational projects of Lydgate and of the narrator. Where scientist and narrator are committed to uncovering the origins of life and removing obstacles to direct understanding and sympathy, Bulstrode is devoted to the promotion of secrecy. His clandestine commercial operations in London consisted of receiving dirty goods, cleansing them, and producing ostensibly clean money. In suppressing the existence of his wife's daughter—Will's mother, as it turns out—he conceals paternity and separates an heir from his fortune. In his rebirth as an upstanding Middlemarch banker he succeeds in acquiring a new set of personal origins and, for a time, in making his settlement in the town seem immemorial. Finally, in controlling the secret strings of credit of the town's business, he uses control over the origins of capital to coerce the actions of those dependent on it. In his systematic obscuring of origins, Bulstrode's life is the image of the ceaseless dynamism of vocation broken free of moral direction and allowed to realize its potential for selfish individualism.

Bulstrode's intimate involvement with religion constitutes an important statement about the excesses inherent in the Calvinist doctrine of the calling. Predestination, to begin with, because it views all events as the expression of God's will, can too easily be used as a justification for withholding action in circumstances where evil is apparent. Thus Bulstrode can comfortably rationalize his failure to locate his first wife's daughter with the thought that her estrangement was providentially ordained. Predestination further implies that the elect are only "vessels" or "instruments" of a larger purpose. Since Bulstrode is utterly convinced of his own election, he believes that his calling permits him to use others in an instrumental way; for he is merely giving the less fortunate an opportunity to carry out his will, which, unlike theirs, is providentially directed. Thus Bulstrode has no qualms about making use of Lydgate, first for the new hospital and then for covering up the banker's complicity in Raffles' death.

Bulstrode's exploitation of others is facilitated by the traditional attitude of the Calvinist saint toward the nonelect. "This consciousness of divine grace of the elect and holy," Weber writes, "was accompanied by an attitude toward the sin of one's neighbor, not of sympathetic understanding based on consciousness of one's own weakness, but of hatred and contempt for him as an enemy of God bearing the signs of eternal damnation."[16] With this attitude Bulstrode covers a multitude of sins, culminating in Raffles' being allowed to die; for his death is the fitting end of a man who is already spiritually damned.

Finally, according to the symbolic code of the novel,

Bulstrode's life brings together two of the most reprehensible tendencies depicted in *Middlemarch:* the tendency of religion to leave human concerns behind by becoming totally otherworldly, and the tendency of business to lose contact with objects in favor of exchanges based on pure capital, that is, finance. In the mutual reinforcement of otherworldliness and pure finance, George Eliot saw the ultimate bankruptcy of the historical form of the Calvinist idea of calling.

Bulstrode again illustrates that vocation in *Middlemarch,* both as an idea and as a life project, is deeply problematic. As the new vehicle of ennoblement, vocational aspiration signifies the urge to contribute to the world's advancement, to press the implications of knowledge and discovery, to relieve the weight of misery and oppression — and all this through a course of action that allows man to realize and objectify himself through his labors. Yet as a self-consuming ambition promising redemption, vocation is also a dangerously modern legitimation of egotism and self-aggrandizement, isolating its practitioner and laying waste those around him. In so unflinchingly representing both the possibilities and costs of the mobile individualism released by the newly industrializing society, George Eliot suggests that both sides of vocation are essentially aspects of the same urge and, therefore, both destined to be rooted in the same person. It is the particular achievement of *Middlemarch* that, rather than distributing the contradictions of vocation among the novel's cast of characters, they are installed complete with each of several complex figures. The novel's portrayal of characters who are deeply divided yet always identifiable — Dorothea as autocratic philanthropist and as martyred savior is, always, unmistakably Dorothea — is an effective representation of the operation of a divided yet unitary social force.

7

DANIEL DERONDA AND THE

MESSIANIC CALLING

If character in *Middlemarch* is constituted as a totality in which contradictions are integrated rather than dispersed, in *Daniel Deronda* the picture is different. The vocational impulse is decisively split into "good" ambition and "bad" ambition, yielding a selflessly beatific Deronda and a willfully ruthless Gwendolen. Deronda's messianic longing to do something great for his people seems more like an inexhaustible natural resource than an ambition whose origins are in the needs of the self. Opposed to Deronda's elevation, Gwendolen's ambition stands as an emblem of pure will, a metaphor of mobility stripped of all pretense of benevolent intention. Writing four years after the composition of *Middlemarch* and writing of a contemporary postreform era forty years beyond the action of that novel, George Eliot could no longer conceive of a society in which the demonic and noble aspects of vocation could be joined. To remain in society of necessity involves becoming a Gwendolen; and to become a Daniel, society—at least English society—had to be left behind.

Standing over the roulette table in the novel's stunning opening scene, Gwendolen's pose is emblematic of her later career: a desperate, inflexible will trained on an uncontrollable moving object. Gwendolen's play at the tables is essentially aristocratic in style: she reminds us of the gamblers of *Middlemarch*. She abandons herself to the excitement of rapid accumulation and loss, playing, she believes, with surplus capital whose loss will not affect the quality or station of her life. That same night Gwendolen is informed in a letter from her mother that the entire family fortune has been lost in the failure of the enormous joint-stock concern of Grapnell & Co., and that she and her sisters will henceforth have to live on the charity of an uncle who, although similarly ruined, has a clerical living to fall back on. *Daniel Deronda* thus begins with the decline of one morally repugnant form of risk and the ascendancy of a far more frightening one. Rudely plunged into this new world of risk, the rational speculation of wager capitalism, Gwendolen must leave off playing for pleasure and begin the deadly earnest business of systematically risking for gain.

Submitting to a lower station in life means accepting the humiliation of dependence, and this Gwendolen is not willing to do. In order to restore the free play of her will, she is determined instead to parlay her "nonliquid" resources (beauty, manners, and, she believes, theatrical talent) into financial security. For a woman with these endowments, the conventional way to accomplish this goal is through marriage, but for Gwendolen marriage signifies no escape from bondage. She wonders "whether she could not achieve substantiality for herself and know gratified ambition without bondage" (ch. 23, p. 295).[1] With the idea of a career of her own in mind, she asks the London impresario Herr Klesmer how quickly she could train as a singer for the stage. Klesmer tells her flatly that the world of art operates according to a strict vocational ethic that judges aspirants solely on the basis of achieved merit. The beauty and manners that

Gwendolen has counted on to give her power over polite society would no longer be of any use. Music and art, Klesmer avers, are "higher vocations" in which the patient suppression of self is the only road to eventual artistic realization. Moreover, since Gwendolen lacks true genius (she is the first to admit it), the most she could hope to achieve, even with rigorous training, would be a kind of modest accomplishment. For Gwendolen, this is hardly promising.

With vocation out of the picture, Gwendolen chooses to marry and accepts Grandcourt's proposal. Although Grandcourt's cruelty is no surprise to the reader, in terms of Gwendolen's expectations it is painfully ironic. The course of action she hoped would deliver her from dependence and humiliation becomes an ordeal of unimaginable debasement and subjugation. The contest between Grandcourt and Gwendolen unfolds at the level of pure will; there are no "issues" between them other than the granting or denial of personal liberty. Although on her own part Gwendolen had certainly always been willful, her willfulness had been of the selfish sort which, in its eagerness to please itself, was unkind to others. In Grandcourt's desire to possess his wife's soul, however, there is a willfulness of an entirely different order: a radical intentionality toward evil. This is the first such occurrence in George Eliot's writings. In her earlier treatment of unsympathetic characters (one thinks of Arthur Donnithorne, Mrs. Transome, Bulstrode) there is no principle which, aside from the unintentional consequences of selfish acts, by itself brings evil into the world. On the contrary, the characteristic moment in her fiction is the convulsive realization *after the fact* that the alluvial deposits of evil that was not at first intended have hardened into an enormous, unmovable fact.

The gratuitousness of Grandcourt's cruelty vitiates the conventions of George Eliot's fiction in another way. It tears a rent in the carefully achieved naturalism of the earlier novels, and through this new opening there rushes a proces-

sion of demonic images. Cursed jewels, secret compart-
ments, images of serpent women and reptilian men, ocular
possession and existential terror—these figures from the
shadow world of enchantment are uneasy presences for
the experienced reader of George Eliot. To work them into
the fabric of this novel it is necessary to take the unusual
measure of turning to the motifs of folklore: Gwendolen is at
times a princess in exile and a queen dethroned. This departure from naturalism is not an insignificant moment in
George Eliot's literary career, a career which as early as
Scenes of Clerical Life committed itself to the Feuerbachian
project of secularization and disenchantment. The goal had
been to humanize fully the work of literature by letting it
reveal the human meanings of supernatural symbols and the
human agency behind predetermined behavior.

The space in which Grandcourt and Gwendolen move
is obviously no longer susceptible to such humanization. It
remains lodged between an unrecoverable transcendent
meaning and a humanized meaning that has been forfeited
or driven out. Precisely here, in the void between God and
man, the *daimon* was thought by antiquity to operate. In
Daniel Deronda we encounter principles of absolute evil
which, lacking in explanation and motivation, seem demon-
like as they work their own furious logic. The only part of
the novel protected from demonism—the uncontaminated
and "clean" space—is the part detached from upper-middle-class English society. This is the "other" half of the
novel, Deronda's half. The sign of this difference, I would
like to argue, is the continued receptivity in the novel of
Deronda and the Jewish people to the call of high vocations.
As disciplined work toward a high purpose, vocation is the
exemplary model of life in the humanized world. However,
it is subject to the same imaginative radicalization as the
values of English society. Just as the ambition and willfulness
of Gwendolen and Grandcourt are demonized, Deronda's
ambition for the good is idealized and, as we shall see, this

idealization proceeds almost to the point where it attains to the transcendent authority it had replaced, to the myths of the hero and the savior.

The nature of Deronda's decision to decline involvement in English society is made clear early in the novel in his decision to decline pursuing Gwendolen. His guardian, Sir Hugo, has been urging him to try to "cut out" Grandcourt.

> "Are you inclined to run after her?"
>
> "On the contrary," said Deronda, "I should rather be inclined to run away from her."
>
> "Why, you would easily cut out Grandcourt. A girl with her spirit would think you the finer match of the two," said Sir Hugo, who often tried Deronda's patience by finding a joke in impossible advice. (A difference of taste in jokes is a great strain of the affections.)
>
> "I suppose pedigree and land belong to a fine match," said Deronda, coldly.
>
> "The best horse will win in spite of pedigree, my boy. You remember Napoleon's *mot—Je suis un ancêtre*," said Sir Hugo, who habitually undervalued birth, as men dining well often agree that the good of life is distributed with wounderful equality.
>
> "I am not sure that I want to be an ancestor," said Deronda. "It doesn't seem to me the rarest sort of origination."
>
> "You won't run after the pretty gambler, then?" said Sir Hugo, putting down his glasses.
>
> "Decidedly not."
>
> This answer was perfectly truthful; nevertheless it had passed through Deronda's mind that under other circumstances he should have given way to the interest this girl had raised in him, and tried to know more of her.
>
> (Ch. 17, pp. 201-202)

Sir Hugo's decency, evident here in his affection for Deronda and elsewhere in his supervision of the young man's education, makes him the best of English society as well as Deronda's last remaining bridge to it. Because of his privileged position, his misjudgments in this passage are a particularly grave indication of the state of social opinion in general. In his eyes, for example, Gwendolen's spiritedness makes her worth running after. To Deronda, on the other hand, the prospect of courtship as a game of running after, cutting out, and carrying away, would be disgusting enough even if the woman were worthwhile. The fact that Gwendolen's desirability rests on her spiritedness and beauty alone is a sign of a society in which higher values have been annulled. Gwendolen should be run away from rather than run after. Beyond this, Deronda indicates that Sir Hugo has fundamentally misperceived Gwendolen's motives in allowing herself to be pursued by Grandcourt. In a market society, Deronda implies, a woman who is possessed of *only* beauty and spirit (and lacking an ascetic commitment to ideals) will always choose pedigree and land over sentiment and moral charisma.

Mistakenly believing that Deronda has been disparaging himself with these remarks, Sir Hugo assures him (with a racing image suited to his own idea of Gwendolen as a "pretty gambler") that in the end the best horse will win in spite of birth. With a ready egalitarianism of the comfortable Radical, Sir Hugo quotes Napoleon's *Je suis un ancêtre,* a declaration that can be understood either as "having given birth to myself I am my own ancestor," or "to the lineage that will descend from me I shall be an ancestor." To a young man troubled about the possibility of his own illegitimacy, his guardian's (perhaps his father's) glib dismissal of the importance of birth is bound to be upsetting. The example of Napoleon recommends a career of imperial individualism in which success owes nothing to the past and everything to the power of self-creation. To conquer Gwendolen in this fashion would be to take her like a country and, in so doing, to capitulate to the conscienceless ambition of the society he rejects. Although Deronda is searching for an originating vocation, it does not strike him that the path suggested by Sir Hugo is the "rarest form of origination." He would prefer, in fact, *not* to be his own ancestor, but since he cannot find a desirable paternity in the society around him, he will choose to contintue as an orphan.

At the close of the dialogue, the narrator returns to reveal to the reader what Deronda has not wanted to admit to his guardian in conversation. Despite his decision not to pursue Gwendolen, she has nevertheless affected him in ways he does not wholly understand. He feels an interest in her and an urge "to know more of her." This fascination will never become entirely conscious on the part of the novelist; it prefigures the curious relations between Deronda and Gwendolen later in the novel: the barely suppressed eroticism of the sinner's appeal to her savior and the disdainful, yet involuntary, fascination of the doctor-savior with his corrupt patient.

Meanwhile, Deronda has to decide what vocation to take up. He is told by Sir Hugo that, after coming down from Cambridge, he will have the modest financial independence of a bachelor and the freedom to choose any honorable profession he wishes. Although he is free to become a barrister, a writer, a don, or to take up politics (the clergy and medicine are not mentioned), Sir Hugo confesses that politics would please him the most; he should be highly gratified if Deronda were pulling by his side for the cause of progress (ch. 16, pp. 215-216). After Deronda has been reading law for a time, Sir Hugo returns to the subject. Deronda is extremely articulate in private conversation, and as a result Sir Hugo does not understand why he declines to take up politics as a public vocation. However, Daniel stands his ground. " 'I cannot persuade myself to look at politics as a profession . . . I don't want to make a living out of opinions . . . especially out of borrowed opinions.' " Sir Hugo, without violating his habitual tone of affectionate solicitude, takes great issue with Deronda on the matter. " 'The business of the country must be done . . . And it never could be, my boy, if everybody looked at politics as if they were prophecy, and demanded an inspired profession. If you are to get into Parliament, it won't do to sit still and wait for a call either from heaven or constituents' " (ch. 33, p. 434).

Politics, for Deronda, is much too important to be pursued in the manner of one of the professions as they are conventionally practiced. The disinterestedness with which opinions should be formulated and made public must always be compromised by the exigencies of income, party honor, and popular sentiment. Against what he considers Deronda's overscrupulousness, Sir Hugo bases his protest on the difference between the secular and the prophetic notions of calling. The prophet suffers from no uncertainty as to the origins of his inspiration and the terms of his mission. But it is not prophets, Sir Hugo insists, who are equipped to carry on the business of the country; this is left to politicians, who must discover the call in their own opinions and in their own ambitions for service and who must work toward goals of their own devising. Sir Hugo intends the distinction as a reductio ad absurdum: to oppose the down-to-earth political notion of vocation is to evoke a prophetic model too archaic and supernatural to be taken seriously.

The joke, ironically, is on the good-natured baronet, for it is precisely the prophetic conception of vocation that Deronda considers the less ridiculous. Rather than being, as Sir Hugo suggests, a sign of overscrupulousness on his part, Deronda's rejection of politics as a vocation is a principled negation of the same order of importance as his rejection of Gwendolen. In reaching beyond politics, Deronda is reaching beyond the modes of self-transcendence available in England at the time.

The new self Deronda is reaching for is suggested in an early scene in the novel. Finished with his education and expected to take his place in English society, Deronda has begun (in order to keep himself open for politics) to read law. He does so at the strong suggestion of his guardian, and his resistance to the enterprise allows him to find plenty of time to indulge his "habit of reflexive meditation" by rowing on the Thames. As the sun sets one evening he pulls up on the bank to contemplate the stillness. "He was forgetting everything else in a half-speculative, half-involuntary identification of himself with the objects he was looking at, thinking how far it might be possible habitually to shift his centre till his own personality would be no less outside him than the landscape, —when the sense of something moving on the bank opposite him where it was bordered by a line of willow-bushes, made him turn his glance thitherward" (ch. 17, pp. 228-229). The noise in the willow rushes is the beginning of a suicide attempt by a desperate young Jewess named Mirah. Deronda feverishly rows to the opposite bank, grabs the girl, and assures her that he will die before he lets any harm come to her.

Reflective self-absorption, a cry for help, and a heroic act of salvation — this sequence of events prefigures the later course of Deronda's life. The reflection is *self*-absorbed only in the sense that it takes place in the mind. Reclining with his mind at rest, Deronda does not, like Lydgate, savor the contributions he will make to his profession or, like Dorothea, anticipate the good that will result from the realization of his plans. In fact, he loses all thought of himself in a process of emptying his mind so that the external objects around him become the only contents of consciousness. This reverie is different from the experiences of romantic transcendentalism and contemporary neoidealism in which external reality is produced by the intensity of pure mind. Deronda speculates on the opposite possibility, that the self could be released from its own needs to center completely on the objects of the world.

Eventually, Deronda achieves the complete externalization of which he dreams. The water and sky of the landscape before him are exchanged for the aspirations and destiny of his people. Through his vocation as redeemer, Deronda effects so complete an identification with the Jewish nation that the attributes of his individuality (as far as he can be said to have any) are absorbed in his messianic role. This achievement signals the closing of the ironic space which was the imaginative terrain of *Middlemarch,* that is, the gap between the resisting individuality of the self and the ascetic demands of professional role. Deronda is the new hero who exists as *nothing other* than his vocation.

Deronda's ready sympathy and generosity of mind, however, turn out to be the chief obstacles to his vocational self-realization. He has the opposite problem of most Victorian heroes, whose anguished experience of a world bereft of meaning can be allayed by no amount of feverish activity. For Deronda the world is a plenum whose very fullness threatens the capacity to take meaningful action. His faculty of sympathetic imagination is so finely developed that he habitually "sees things as they probably appear to others" (ch. 32, p. 412), and anticipates the pain that the redress of injustice will work on its perpetrators. Deronda is the perfected Victorian political personality who is as "loathe to part with long-sanctioned forms" as he is "fervidly democratic in his feeling for the multitudes" (ch. 32, p. 413). However commendable Deronda's sensitivities, they do little to help him select one cause that would gather, rather than diffuse, his energies. Too "plenteous" and "flexible," sympathy ends by "falling into the one current" of reflexive contemplation (ch. 32, p. 412).

The most outstanding practitioner of sympathy in the world of George Eliot's fiction is, undoubtedly, the novelist herself. From *Scenes of Clerical Life* onwards, her program of deromanticization required eliciting sympathy for the commonplace, the ugly, the unwanted: not only Felix Holt but also Mrs. Transome, not only Dorothea but also Casaubon. As a redemptive calling, narrative recalls the misjudged and delivers the forgotten. Since, in theory, all things high and low deserve attention, George Eliot's intention implied both a radical nominalism and an absolute democracy, doctrines according to which all particulars of an imaginative universe have equal claims to sympathetic evocation. To respond to each of these claims would obviously lead either to a paralysis like Deronda's or to an endless flow of writing which, lacking any selectivity, would be formless. George Eliot seems to have been conscious of these questions when she wrote in *Middlemarch:* "If we had a keen vision and feeling of all ordinary human life, it would be like hearing the grass grow and the squirrel's heart beat, and we should die of that roar which lies on the other side of silence. As it is, the quickest of us walk about well wadded with stupidity" (ch. 20, p. 144). The either/or here is startling: either the fatal intensity of absolute sympathy or the inert silence of absolute insensibility. The only way out is a partial deafness that muffles the sound of humanity in order to make its noises sufferable, and therefore intelligible. If writing, then, is to give any articulation to human suffering, it must follow this via media by choosing some particulars for accentuation and representation and ignoring the others. Selection turns moral sympathy into narrative art.[2]

Deronda is at the same impasse. His unorganized moral energies are in danger of foundering as Puritan writers predicted would happen to men who did not submit to a "certain calling." Aware of the progressive paralysis of his will, Deronda begins to long for "either some external event, or some inward light, that would urge him into a definite line of action and compress his wandering energies" (ch. 32, p. 413). He seeks a "fixed local habitation" that would justify partiality and partisanship. He seeks what Calvinism says he has a right to expect: a call, either as an outward sign or an inner light. In *Middlemarch* the experience of the call was secularized. Lydgate experiences his affinity for medicine as the sudden growth of an "intellectual passion"; Will and

Fred come to politics and farming more by trial and circumstance than by the disclosure of a distinguishable sign. But
Deronda seeks a sign, and his search, like many of the other
mythologized structures of the novel, recalls the earlier, less
secularized notion of the calling.

When the call finally comes, it is in the form of a disclosure of origins — Deronda discovers that by birth he is a
Jew.[3] (Besides not being a surprise, Deronda's Jewishness is,
in a sense, "achieved" before it is revealed as a birthright,
much in the same way the delightful men and women of
Dickens' early fiction turn out in the end to be cousins,
nephews, and nieces.) Participation in the Jewish nation
offers the gratifications which, in the scheme of George
Eliot's fiction, were once available in premodern England,
in the timeless valleys of Silas Marner's Raveloe or Adam
Bede's Hayslope: family without incestuous violence, historical authority and discipleship, organic community and
fellowship. Most significantly, Deronda's new identity
affords a stage for action on the largest possible scale: not
Dorothea's unhistoric acts of kindness, but nothing less than
a messianic mission on behalf of an entire people. Operating
on this scale, fictional character can obviously no longer be
contained by the premodern novel, which usually confines
itself to the empirical world of middle-class relations. As a
character, moreover, Deronda is so overdetermined that the
genre's ordinary equipment of irony, complexity, and development does not suffice to render him. Since Deronda is
larger than life, his portrayal requires materials that loom
equally as large. Just as Grandcourt and Gwendolen preside
over the demonic side of the novel, Deronda presides over
the realm of the mythic hero. In order to "handle" Deronda,
George Eliot brings a series of heroic figures to bear. A con-
venient example of one of these is evident in the scene of
Mirah's attempted suicide, quoted above. One reading of
the scene and the chain of events it sets in motion might be
as follows. Saving the drowning Jewish child in the bulrushes

by the river, a young Moses unconsciously recapitulates his own origins and unwittingly performs his first saving act for a people he does not yet know to be his own. As an un- awakened Jewish prince in a gentile court, he is instinctively drawn to the suffering of his people even before he is given the explicit charge to liberate them and lead them to the Promised Land. If the text everywhere identified Deronda with Moses, the novel would be an allegory, but there are echoes of other heroes: the prophets of the Bible, Christ, the messiah of Jewish lore, and the figures of medieval romance. Here, at the terminus of George Eliot's career, vocation, in its heroic aspect, becomes the ultimate image of the self.

Deronda's transcendence puts him beyond the prob- lematics of vocation. Since, unlike Lydgate, Deronda *is* his vocation, there is no shadowy overlap where life proceeds beneath and beyond the scrutiny of the vocational code. Fortunately for Deronda, there are no jealous competitors to foul his good intentions and no prosaic conditions of pov- erty to solicit unworthy behavior. In Mirah, moreover, Deronda has been provided with the kind of "good unworldy woman" Farebrother had urged on Lydgate, the kind who will expedite, rather than hamper, the prosecution of voca- tion.

A final word needs to be said about the verbal medium of Deronda's transcendence. The moral brutalization of English middle- and upper-middle-class society is reflected in *Daniel Deronda* in the despiritualization of the language of these classes and their use of language as an instrument of power. Both because of their exclusion from this society and because of the richness of their own traditions, the Jews have retained a privileged relation to the verbal imagination. As subjects that were not commonly thought worthy of artistic representation, the Jews are examples of the novelist's power to reveal the moral beauty of what to secular English society seems only vulgar and retrograde; and in their own right, Jews like Mordecai are capable of prophetic visions that penetrate the frozen surface of society. In *Felix Holt* and *Middlemarch* vision began to be important, but it was reserved (as in Dorothea's all-night vigil) for the one or two moments of climactic breakthrough. In *Daniel Deronda* vision has become the ethos of an entire people, practiced par excellence by its deliverer. To describe Mordecai's eschatological speculations and Deronda's poetic perceptions of the East End and, most of all, his visions of his people's future, George Eliot strains toward a prose that would fuse visionary ideality with concrete objectification. This is obviously a prose which, together with its speaker, is no longer at home in the world of the novel. Like the figure of Deronda itself, it is no longer of this world.

A section from one of Mordecai's speeches is oddly conscious of its own formal impossibility.

> What is needed is the leaven — what is needed is the seed of fire. The heritage of Israel is beating in the pulses of millions; it lives in their veins as a power without understanding, like the morning exultation of herds; it is the inborn half of memory, moving as in a dream among writings on the walls, which it sees dimly but cannot divide into speech. Let the torch of visible community be lit! Let the reason of Israel disclose itself in a great outward deed, and let there be another great migration, another choosing of Israel to be a nationality whose members may still stretch to the ends of the earth, even as the sons of England and Germany, whom enterprise carried afar, but who still have a national hearth and a tribunal of national opinions. Will any say, "It cannot be"?
>
> (Ch. 42, p. 596)

Mordecai is addressing the workingman's club, The Philosophers, on the question of a national homeland for the Jews. His point is that the desire for such a homeland is the unconscious hope of every Jew, part of the inherited memory of the people; and all that is needed to convert this latent energy into a "great outward deed" is the advent of a determined catalyst. The manner of Mordecai's address is deliberate archaism after the style of the prophetic writings of the Old Testament: the elevated exhortatory tone; the rhythmic repetition and heaping up of similes; the collapsed distance between declared possibilities and inevitable outcomes. George Eliot elsewhere states that this language reflects "the passionate current of an ideal life straining to embody itself." Yet instead of ideality, we are most conscious of absence; we miss here the usual gratifications of George Eliot's writing: rationality, the ironic organization of discourse, and a concentration of present complexity rather than potential or future certainty. The rhetorical impossibility of this triumph is rooted in the substance of Mordecai's message. He is, after all, speaking of a power that is not conscious of itself, of an unawakened memory that moves among bits of prophetic writing it cannot yet divide into words. This is a description of the language Mordecai speaks and the language the novelist uses to speak of him: it is a language not yet articulated, not yet ready to be spoken. But George Eliot speaks anyway, and though she would have us take it as a notation of its future inevitability, we read these declarations and visions as signs of a circumstance which is even more inevitable: the growing chasm between the ambitions of language and the matrix of social experience.

The essence of the visionary mode, the novelist tells us, is the capacity to see the world in a series of linked images that point beyond the world. This capacity, furthermore, is conferred on the exiled as a kind of power that arises from their disinherited condition. I repeat these facts because they reveal how *Daniel Deronda* is poised toward later texts in which vision and exile are also powerfully joined, toward the appearance of the artist and the hegemony of art.

8

EPILOGUE: THE CRAFT OF
SOCIETY AND THE
VOCATION OF ART

By putting aside the inter-
connections and contradictions of personal and social relations George Eliot was able to reinvent a religious vision of
the essential unity of imaginative experience and collective
responsibility. Mordecai's visionary speeches and Deronda's
artistic reveries argue for the transformative powers of the
individual mind, while at the same time the contents of
those visions and reveries express an impassioned concern
for the fortunes of the nation is a whole. *Daniel Deronda*
presents the possibility of art's playing a redemptive role in
the life of an unredeemed society, and by offering its characters a role in this process the novel gives them the opportunity to assume vocations of transcendent importance. This
covenant between art and society is a possibility that can be
allowed only on the grounds of religious hope, and the argu-
ment of *Daniel Deronda* makes it clear that, without its
theistic and dogmatic forms, religion has indeed been
smuggled back in after its varied displacements in George
Eliot's earlier work. The rebirth of the individual into the

mystic body of the nation, the endowment of prophecy, the nonultimacy of physical reality, the sense of an advancing higher purpose in the affairs of men — George Eliot's desperate version of the Ruskinian moral aesthetic cannot hold without considerable support from another order of explanation and value. The sanction of religion is indispensable; without it, behind the wishful vision of mutual fruitfulness, the growing antagonism between art and society would be laid bare.

The literary fate of the idea of vocation in the remaining years of the century is the story of a twin defection from the high compact of *Daniel Deronda.* In the literature of the 1880s and 1890s art and society break free of the reinvented religious convenant and embark on separate paths; with their separation, the idea of vocation also splits and proceeds along two separate tracks. To exemplify the new kind of vocation afforded by new social and historical aims I wish to adduce the figure of Beatrice Webb in her autobiography *My Apprenticeship,* and for the new vocation afforded by art the figure of Stephen Dedalus in James Joyce's *A Portrait of the Artist as a Young Man.* Although *My Apprenticeship* and *Portrait of the Artist* are very much twentieth-century documents, I am concerned here with the way in which they sum up and reflect upon the experience of the end of the previous century.

My Apprenticeship was first published in 1926, but the bulk of the book consists of diary entries from the 1880s and 1890s and covers the years of Beatrice Webb's life as a young woman. Though completed in Trieste in 1916, *Portrait of the Artist* was begun in Dublin in 1904 and similarly deals with the last two decades of the nineteenth century.

Stephen Dedalus and Beatrice Webb do not so much divorce themselves from religion as appropriate its passion, discipline, and sanction. George Gissing's *New Grub Street* (1891) and Hale White's Mark Rutherford novels (1881 and later) illustrate what becomes of the conditions of work when the separation from religion is sudden or total and when the fruits of an easy secularization are not available. *New Grub Street*[1] is a world in which the profession of writing exists at the farthest remove from the priestly men of letters in Carlyle's heroic pantheon and from the privileged authority of the narrator of *Middlemarch*. The producers of literary objects are not ennobled by the least residue of the idea of vocation; they write to eat. Their books enjoy no value beyond what they bring in money or reputation. The world of letters is the world of the market, in which no religious meaning, however transvalued, elevates the system of economic relations.

Mark Rutherford,[2] the hero of Hale White's series of autobiographical novels, would hold on to that meaning if he could, but its loss means permanent alienation from the generative energies of life and vocation. Rutherford is a dissenting minister who, after losing his orthodox faith, can neither adopt a new system nor put aside religious questions altogether. He is haunted by the thought of death, "the cessation is vacancy of the noblest men and women," yet he can neither be convinced by the Christian idea of the immortality of the personality nor consoled by the humanist idea of the immortality of noble actions shared by George Eliot in "The Choir Invisible." So with the thought of God: he could never "in the least degree reconcile what he thought he ought to believe about God with the actual apparently cruel facts of nature." The acute sense of living at a time after the passing of the old order and before the rise of a new one, when no certainty could be hoped for, casts a pall of nervous agitation and morbidity over Rutherford's life. The modest affirmation he eventually wins for himself involves less the resolution of these tensions than the blunting of their force.[3] Only when Rutherford finally accepts the insolubility of the moral problem and the unavailability of an adequate system of explanation does he gain some release from anxiety and permit himself some of the smaller pleasures of life.

In *The Autobiography of Mark Rutherford,* as in nearly all the works in this genre, there is a single occupational situation: a young man headed for the clergy loses faith and declines to take orders, or a minister's convictions force him to leave the ministry and he then searches for some way to reconstruct his life. In Rutherford's case the reconstruction never takes place; he remains eviscerated. Though he becomes a parliamentary reporter, having lost the ministry, his work is robbed of vocational power and becomes a temporizing device.

In contrast, Robert Elsmere, the hero of one of the most widely read novels of the period, comes through his ordeal of faith nearly untouched.[4] Elsmere is an Anglican minister of intellectual temperament who leaves the comfort of an Oxford life for parish work as a country rector. What engages him most is not the teaching of the faith in the weekly sermon but the chance to relieve human misery. When he sees that the villages and tenant farms belonging to the local squire have fallen into an appalling and dangerous state of disrepair, he wages a successful battle against the squire's hardness of heart, while personally caring for the stricken victims of the abuses. Victorious in social reform, Elsmere loses to the squire on the score of religious faith. His conversations with the squire, an erudite philosophical skeptic conversant with the latest German thought, expose him to the developmental hypothesis and test his faith on the question of Christian testimony and evidence. Deeply affected, Elsmere realizes that he can no longer be true to his office and resigns the ministry. He settles in London and throws himself into slum work in the East End. Gradually regaining his intellectual equilibrium, he learns to live without supernatural assurances and begins to develop a view of Christianity centered around identification with the sufferings of the historical Jesus. When he dies of a tubercular infection contracted in his work, Elsmere stands at the head of the New Brotherhood of Christ, a fellowship that crosses class lines to draw men together in the betterment of society through the inspiration of, if not the belief in, Christ.

What is striking in Elsmere's career is that after all the crisis, agony, and upheaval, he continues to do essentially the same thing he did before his break with the church. If the subjects of his preaching have changed and the role in which he serves the poor is no longer a pastoral one, the nature of his activity remains unchanged. From the beginning Mrs. Ward gives us a humanized priest practicing a kind of Feuerbachian Christianity; so we experience no great dislocation when the function continues, although the ecclesiastical connection has been dropped. The novelist takes it for granted that the baton has long been passed from the priest to the social worker and social reformer. We are meant to see a transfer of power here, though we must view it as paradoxical: the new social callings can be efficacious only if they are divorced from supernatural religion, yet their patrilineal association with the aura of the priesthood is necessary to give the new callings legitimacy.

In Beatrice Webb's autobiography *My Apprenticeship* the transfer has gone so far to the side of society that there is no lingering doubt as to the worthiness of human affairs rather than spiritual matters as the object of ameliorative energies. The study of society can make claims on its own behalf, not just because it is the humanized form of a religious idea or obligation. But there is a price for this final disentanglement from religious sanctions: those sanctions cannot be evoked to make the work more glorious than it is. The investigation of society, Beatrice Webb insists, is a craft and not a vocation. She chooses, moreover, to tell the story of her coming into her craft in a purely autobiographical form, rejecting such equivocating semi-genres as the *roman à thèse* of *Robert Elsmere* or the thinly disguised autobiographical novel of the Rutherford series. She is aware that she is writing something other than a novel and that her life

171

experience compels a different frame of self-explanation. Her attitude to the novel is a good point of departure for understanding her relationship both to such works of fiction of an earlier generation as *Middlemarch* and to such novels to come (from the point of view of her diary) as *A Portrait of the Artist.*

In discussing her disillusionment with and eventual defection from the self-confident positivism of Henry Spencer, Beatrice Webb remarks: "For any detailed description of the complexity of human nature, of the variety and mixture in human motive, of the insurgence of instinct in the garb of reason, of the multifarious play of social environment on the individual ego and of the individual ego on the social environment, I had to turn to novelists and poets, to Fielding and Flaubert, to Balzac and Browning, to Thackeray and Goethe."[5] The ommission of George Eliot is a curious one, for the similarities of concern and even of cadence are striking: probing the complexity of human motives, revealing the variety of character, exposing the dissimulations of desire, investigating the interplay of self with surroundings. It is as though the wise narrative intelligence of *Middlemarch* were addressing to the reader a reverie on the glories of the narrative vocation. Beatrice Webb despairs of the availability of such intelligence; social analysis in the mode of Spencer has developed no psychology adequate to explain individual social existence. She has therefore turned in the direction of what she will eventually call "social investigation," a craft that attempts to study the larger, collective influences of social institutions and declines the study of individual personality. Beatrice Webb writes of a time at the end of the nineteenth century when a transfer of responsibilities is taking place between two modes of discourse. The high responsibility narrative prose fiction has borne for the critical representation of social existence and social institutions is being exchanged for a preoccupation with individual consciousness and individual behavior in extreme situations. Concurrently, social analysis, which had hitherto displayed the wider concerns characteristic of the Ruskinian moral aesthetic, now becomes a more disciplined and methodic tool for taking on the task of which the novel is disburdening itself.

If Dorothea Brooke is a latter-day St. Theresa, as she is described in the "Prologue" to *Middlemarch,* then Beatrice Webb might be said to be a latter-day Dorothea. The two women display a strongly similar constellation of ambitions and anxieties. As a young woman, Beatrice Webb longs desperately for self-development and self-expression, for access to sources of profound and effectual knowledge, for the privilege of contributing to the progress of humanity, for the fame accruing from writing "a book that would be read." And her ambitions are matched by her doubts: harrowing self-questioning about the "minuteness of her faculties" and about why she "should be born with so much aspiration . . . and with such a beggarly allowance of power wherewith to do it" (p. 137). On the other hand, she is keenly susceptible to the "conventional calls of family duty, reinforced by the prompting of personal vanity and social ambition" (p. 115). The responsibilities of keeping house for her father after her mother's death, the domesticizing pressures of seven married sisters, and the secret complicity of her own heart urge her to take her place in the polite society of the leisured class and thereby relieve her guilt for not being a proper daughter and a prospective wife and mother.

Beatrice Webb, however, came of age at a time of intellectual currents and professional possibilities distinctly different from those available to Dorothea (or to her creator, for that matter). The fundamentalisms from which Beatrice Webb sought release in the 1880s had been the models of religious progress forty years earlier. George Eliot —to speak for a moment in simplified terms—had rejected the strict, pietistic Calvinism of her adolescence for the religion of humanity and the cult of science. It was just these new "religions" which having later become received dogma in liberal circles, had to be demystified by Beatrice Webb before she could create and practice her chosen craft. Many of the leading minds of Britain, supported by a wave of popular enthusiasm, believed that "it was by science, and by science alone, that all human misery would be ultimately swept away," and many, like Spencer, were eager to see the behavior of societies directly in light of discoveries pertaining to natural phenomena (*My Apprenticeship,* p. 126). Beatrice Webb had to reject the specious analogy between society and nature and to winnow the inflated claims of science in order to extract a modest yet vigorous method of observation and hypothesis. The glorification of science was an element in the other rival for Beatrice Webb's higher loyalties: Comtism and the religion of humanity. She welcomes and accepts the transfer in her age of "the impulse of selfsubordinating service . . . consciously and overtly, from God to man" (p. 138); but she eventually rejects the deification of society, "the pitiful attempt by poor humanity to turn its head around and worship its tail" (p. 145). A reverence for humanity is a necessary conviction of any such worker as a social investigator, but regarding humanity as a religious apotheosis rather than a humanly generated ideal results in self-serving ineffectuality.[6]

The "passionate search for a creed" could then proceed to the acquisition of a craft. Beatrice Webb insists on the term "craft" rather than "profession," "calling," or "vocation." Having declined to become a priestess in the cult of science or a communicant in the religion of humanity, she is eager to disassociate her work from redemptive pretensions. It is neither a divinely inspired mission nor a voyage of dramatic discovery and invention. It is a craft, the skillful application of specialized techniques.

The fact that her craft might be modest in relation to the world does not prevent it from playing a saving role in the economy of her own life. Work becomes so essential to her sense of well-being that at the age of twenty-eight (1886) when she is forced to retire from London to care for her father after a stroke, she undergoes a period of severe mental crisis, one not dissimilar to that of Teufelsdröckh and Mill. Deprived of the "narcotic of work," she finds abstinence tormenting. Depressive, suicidal thoughts invade her mind. She wonders how far she is susceptibile of altruistic motives and how far she is "prey to passion, self-consciousness and egotism." Until then she had prided herself in her capacity to accomplish productive work without the necessity or mediation of a husband (Dorothea Brooke is greatly different in this), but now she wonders whether her frenetic social work is merely an avoidance of the "usefulness of wifehood and motherhood." Slowly, the deadpoint in her career is put behind her. She reaches a provisional acceptance of the inconstancy of her motives; a letter from a newspaper editor encourages her with a modicum of recognition (how like George Eliot of her to tease: "Not a love letter, dear reader, but a prosaic communication from the Editor of the *Pall Mall Gazette*"!). While reading during her forced retreat, she discovers that she has ideas of her own about the methodology of the social sciences, such questions as the right relation of personal observation to statistical inquiry, and she thus begins her first essays in social theory. Finally, her studies in the unregulated oppression of immigrant laborers in London, which she pursues through the new technique of participant observation, come to full recognition when she is asked to testify before the House of Lords Committee on the Sweating System in 1888.

The abundance of recognition she receives at this time arouses nearly as much self-doubt as its scarcity several years earlier. She experiences a "growing distrust of a self-absorbed life and the egotism of successful work, done on easy terms and reaping more admiration than it deserves" (p. 397). As a corrective, Beatrice Webb allows the "resolute, patient affection" of the socialist Sidney Webb to draw her into a marital union. Their union is not so much a marriage as an incorporation of two like-minded reformers. Unlike romantic and bourgeois marrigaes, which demand surrender of independence and activity, their union, she stresses, would be a partnership permitting the more efficient achievement of the goals they hold in common; they would be the "firm of Webb and Webb" whose efficiency would be based on an identity of interests and complementary talents. "I am an investigator," she writes as if on a prospectus, "and he the executant: A considerable work should be the result if we use our combined talents with a deliberate and persistent purpose" (p. 398). It was only after successfully seeking a creed and then acquiring a craft that Beatrice Webb would consider marriage, and then marriage only as a partnership. Their union, so reminiscent of the Puritan conception of marriage as a joint business for the achievement of salvation, has about it also a ring prophetic of the ascetic marriages that are a hallmark of twentieth-century revolutionary movements.

In her diary of 1887, Beatrice Webb writes of the time she began to practice her craft in earnest. "Now that observation is my work I find it necessary to keep two books. . . . Otherwise the autobiography is eaten up by statistics of wages, hours of work, interviews with employers and workpeople — no space for the history of a woman's life" (p. 271). Marriage to Sidney signifies to Beatrice Webb permission to close that private book which is always on the verge of being engulfed; the record of their life together, told in *Our Partnership,* is purely the record of their activities as socialists and reformers. The personal margin is eliminated. *My Apprenticeship* is an impressive document of a double-entry imagination, and in its determination to tell two stories with equal fidelity it comes as close as any biographical or autobiographical enterprise to illuminating the social and individual matrix of the self.

In the past, it was left to the novel to attempt to combine the two: to write the *one* book of the social imagination.

That is the achievement of *Middlemarch,* an achievement based on the premise that inner life and public action are interrelated and that this interrelationship can be represented. At a certain moment this premise obviously ceases to be true, and the writer must make choices. As Beatrice Webb was sealing the diary of her life as a woman and beginning the exclusive account of her career as a socialist, other writers were making different choices.

For those who drew away from the question of society, the search for personal authenticity took its most characteristic shape in a cluster of concerns centered on self-expression, interior consciousness, aesthetic sensibility, and the life of the artist. The imagination, in short, came more and more to be preoccupied with itself. This tendency was already a pronounced feature of *Middlemarch;* in reflections on the shortcomings of the characters and the failure of their projects for discovery, reform, and philanthropy, the novelist was always clearly in mind as the only figure in the novel capable of succeeding in these same enterprises — and not just in some but in all. In *Daniel Deronda,* as we have noted, some of the visionary intensity preserved for the novelist is vouchsafed to her characters; to Mordecai, of course, but also to Deronda, whose imagination holds in mind a visionary future for his people.

Toward the end of the century these concerns become manifest in such phenomena as aestheticism, bohemianism, Whistler's cultural politics, and the reverberations of the French Art for Art's sake. Within the novel proper the signs are also there: James's investigations into the autonomy of sensibility in *The Portrait of a Lady* and his artist tales of the nineties; Conrad's shifting of representation from existential action to the act of narration in *Lord Jim* and *The Heart of Darkness;* Pater's explorations of changing states of impressionistic consciousness in *Marius the Epicurean;* Wilde's claims for the victimizing autonomy of art in *The Picture of Dorian Grey.* As the artist emerges as an ineluctible theme of modern fiction, the awareness of the problematic conditions of that vocation becomes painfully acute: alienation from biological life, the moral snares, the potential vampirage of art, the burden of exile. In its unrelenting naturalistic depiction of the wrecked lives of writers, *New Grub Street* stands at one extreme in which there is no possibility of transcendence. Joyce stands at the other.

In *A Portrait of the Artist as a Young Man* Joyce establishes the vocation of art in a new zone of freedom. Once the prospect of recreating the social world is renounced in favor of the full sufficiency of language, vocation becomes an unparalleled vehicle of transcendence. *A Portrait of the Artist* ends with the same sense of rapture about the possiblities of vocation that *Middlemarch* began with. The scientist and the reformer, however, have been joined in the artist, and their medium — action and knowledge — has become instead the symbolic representation of action and knowledge. With its renewal and transvaluation in Joyce's fiction, the idea of vocation is launched on a new career, as it were, in a newly secured imaginative space.

Like George Eliot, Joyce is concerned with the "moment of vocation," the moment in which the self seizes its identity by a passionate commitment to particular work. In the case of Lydgate, the revelatory experience is quickly dispatched in order to proceed with the main story of vocational maturity and its entanglements. In *A Portrait of the Artist,* however, the moment of vocation concludes the novel; it is what is worked up to, what is achieved, the novel's *telos.* It is a sign that Joyce has enough confidence in his life's work to view its inauguration in terms only partially ironic; unlike Lydgate, *he* has forced the momentary event into a continuing process, and his success enables him to look back from the position of achieved artisthood to a moment which he can authorize to stand for his life as a whole.

Like *Middlemarch,* the achievement of vocation in *A Portrait of the Artist* is the result of a massive act of negation. As Lydgate resisted the self-gratifying irrationality of contemporary medical practice and as Dorothea, for a time, resisted soft-headed notions about a woman's capabilities, so Stephen must resist the father, Dublin, and the church. Each wants to absorb him, to humble him, and to make him serve, but, unlike Lydgate and Dorothea, Stephen makes his refusal stand. Like them, Stephen is trying to escape to a new order of value, the order of vocation; yet, whereas they were confined to the social world, Stephen can be reborn into the radiant family of art. Having nowhere else to go, they succumbed to the solicitations of the world, while Stephen finds a portal in the discovery of the secret powers of language. The discovery of language not only gives Stephen an alternative to the biological order of the family and to the social order of institutions, it provides him with an instrument for exploiting, for his own purposes, the very things he has rejected. As an artist in exile, he will recreate in words what he has rejected in life; father, Dublin, church, once hungry for the soul of the young artist, will now be made to submit to the uses of his imagination.

At the end of chapter IV the director of the Jesuit college summons Stephen and asks him, "Have you ever felt you had a vocation?" (p. 157).[7] "To receive that call," the priest tells him, "is the greatest honor the Almighty God can bestow on a man" (pp. 158-159). No one has the priest's power, given by God, to "bind and loose from sin," to exorcize, to transubstantiate; no man can attain to his "secret knowledge" and his "secret power." Stephen is powerfully tempted by the priest, but as he drifts through the streets of Dublin to the sea, he realizes that the profane call of life is stronger than the voice of the priest. He will indeed have a vocation; it will be in the service of an exalted call; it will require ascetic exile from the company and pleasures of men; it will offer secret knowlede and the power to transform the world. It will, in short, be a priesthood, but a priesthood of the imagination. Though the "text" this priest reads will be new, the function of his vocation will be the same: "he will transmute the daily bread of life into the sacrament of art." Priest, priest of the imagination, artist—this change itself seems to be a transubstantiation.

The ascendant figure of the artist constitutes an important moment in a process of resacrilization: a return to the world of Milton and Wordsworth from which George Eliot had departed. The original Calvinist doctrine of calling was founded upon a secularization of the notion that one could be called to God's service only by withdrawal from worldly pursuits into a priesthood or a monastery; the idea of social vocation employed by George Eliot was in turn founded upon a secularization of the Calvinist teaching that it was God (and not society, or nature) who did the calling. Because Joyce could recover the premodern, even pre-Protestant, roots of vocation, vocation could be continued not merely as a craft, as it was for Beatrice Webb, but as an exalted, redemptive calling. In Joyce, the idea of the calling evokes the earliest sacral associations. The realm of art, like the word of God, is indeed a transcendent order that summons the artist from beyond rather than from within; and to undertake this sacred service the artist must of necessity withdraw from the world and its entrapments.

Rather than merely surviving, the idea of a vocation in *A Portrait of the Artist* is apotheosized. It overshadows all. Exalted in a mythical space beyond the world, vocation is no longer concerned with the moral temptations of aestheticism, the irreconcilability of craft and imagination, the snares of egotism, the encroachments of society. *A Portrait of the Artist* is a brief moment which does not manage to be perpetuated in quite the same way by *Ulysses,* and certainly not in any of the classics of modernism.

> . . . he seemed to hear the noise of dim waves and to see a winged form flying above the waves and slowly climbing the air . . . Was it . . . a prophecy of the end he had been

born to serve and had been following through the mists of childhood and boyhood, a symbol of the artist forging anew in his workshop out of the sluggish matter of the earth a new soaring impalpable imperishable being?

(P. 169)

For an instant the oracles which George Eliot had deciphered are overturned by Joyce's symbolic assertion, and vocation becomes what it had never before been: pure, sacred flight.

NOTES

1. Ideas and Institutions

1. Walter E. Houghton, *The Victorian Frame of Mind* (New Haven: Yale University Press, 1957), p. 242.

2. See Thomas Carlyle, *Past and Present,* bk. 3, ch. 11. Also see John Ruskin's glorification of the medieval worker in *The Stones of Venice,* vol. II, ch. 6, "The Nature of Gothic" (1853).

3. See Max Weber's discussion of the philological background of the concept in his notes to ch. 3 in the English version translated by Talcott Parsons in 1930, *The Protestant Ethic and the Spirit of Capitalism,* 2nd ed. (New York: Charles Scribner's Sons, 1958), beginning on p. 204. *Die protestantische Ethik und der Geist des Kapitalismus* was first published in the *Archiv für Sozialwissenschaft und Sozialpolitik,* vols. 20 and 21, for 1904-05. It was first reprinted in 1920 as the first volume in the series *Gesammelte Aufsatze zur Religion-soziologie.*

4. Ibid., p. 80.

5. The two terms, though largely interchangeable in later writing, have acquired fields of meaning that do not entirely coincide. Because of its Latin provenance, "vocation" retains more echoes of its partial original identification with the priestly office. For these differences, see the *OED.*

6. *Westminster Convention,* quoted in Weber, p. 101.

7. See the chapter on vocational choice in Edmund S. Morgan, *The Puritan Family,* rev. ed. (New York: Harper & Row, 1966).

8. Samuel Hieron, quoted in Michael Walzer, *The Revolution of the Saints* (Cambridge, Mass.: Harvard University Press, 1965), p. 211.

9. Ibid., p. 80.

10. John Bunyan, *The Pilgrim's Progress . . .,* ed. J. B. Wharey, 2nd ed., rev. Roger Sharrock (London: Oxford University Press, 1960), p. 8.

11. Christopher Hill, *The World Turned Upside Down* (New York: Viking Press, 1972), p. 246.

12. On the "professional" nature of politics, see Weber's essay "Politics as a Vocation" in *From Max Weber,* ed. and trans. H. H. Garth and C. Wright Mills (New York: Oxford University Press, 1946), pp. 77-129.

13. The later stages of professional organization are best described by W. J. Reader, *Professional Men* (New York: Basic Books, 1966), a work which impressively updates and revises the major study in the field by A. M. Carr-Saunders and P. A. Wildon, *The Professions* (London: Oxford University Press, 1933). On recent work in the sociology of professionalization, see George Ritzer, *Man and His Work* (New York: Appleton-Century-Croft, 1972), ch. 2, and Howard M. Vollmers and Donald L. Mills, eds., *Professionalization* (Englewood Cliffs, N.J.: Prentice-Hall, 1966). The particular case of the medical profession will be taken up later in connection with Lydgate's career.

14. Graeme Duncan, *Marx and Mill* (Cambridge: Cambridge University Press, 1973), p. 79.

15. *Capital,* vol. I (New York: International Publishers, 1967), p. 763.

2. The Shape of a Life in Biography and Autobiography

1. *Sartor Resartus,* Centenary ed. (London: Chapman and Hall, 1896), p. 125. Subsequent quotations are from this edition. *Sartor Resartus* first appeared in *Fraser's Magazine,* beginning in November 1833. *Middlemarch,* ed. Gordon S. Haight (Boston: Houghton Mifflin Company, 1956), "Epilogue," pp. 612-613. Subsequent quotations are from this edition. *Middlemarch* was first published in eight parts between 1871 and 1872.

2. Recent useful studies of biography and autobiography include: A. O. J. Cockshut, *Truth to Life: The Art of Biography in the Nineteenth Century* (New York: Harcourt Brace Jovanovich, 1974); John N. Morris, *Versions of the Self* (New York: Basic Books, 1966); Roy Pascal, *Design and Truth in Autobiography* (Cambridge, Mass.: Harvard University Press, 1960); James Olney, *Metaphors of Self* (Princeton: Princeton University Press, 1972); Joseph W. Reed, *English Biography in the Early Nineteenth Century* (New Haven: Yale University Press, 1966).

3. The multiple volumes of Carlyle's biography of Frederick VIII are

NOTES TO PAGES 31-64

eloquent later testimony to the impossibility — and the interminability —
of writing a "life."

4. Quotations are from the edition of C. F. Harrold (New York:
Longmans, Green & Co., 1947).

5. Several paragraphs in the *Apologia,* it is true, concern earlier
memories; they record Newman's early predisposition to believe in the
reality of immaterial objects. He wished, he recalls, that the Arabian
Tales were true, and he believed in the existence of angels and in the possibility that he himself might be a hidden angel. But essentially Newman
believed in the reality of only two things: his self and his God. Like Mill's
Autobiography, the *Apologia* is a work about education, but since Newman believed as strongly in self and God at the beginning of his life as at
its end, his education took the form of discovering ever more consistent
doctrinal expressions of that belief. Mill, on the other hand, is true to his
belief in psychological associationism in presenting his life as an empty
container that becomes filled with contents over which he exercises only
limited control.

6. *On Heroes, Hero-Worship and the Heroic in Literature,* Centenary
ed. (London: Chapman and Hall, 1896). Subsequent quotations are from
this edition. The contents of the book were first given as lectures in 1840.

7. Thomas Parker Hughes, ed., *Selections from the Lives of the
Engineers* (Cambridge, Mass: M.I.T. Press, 1966).

8. *The Autobiography of Charles Darwin, 1809-1882,* ed. Nora Bar-
low (New York: W. W. Norton & Co., 1958).

9. *Autobiography of John Stuart Mill,* ed. John Jacob Coss (New York:
Columbia University Press, 1948).

10. The point should not be stressed overmuch. Mill's crisis was certainly a "deconversion" from the religion of Benthamism.

11. One is reminded in this context of the example of Matthew
Arnold, whose vocation as a critic and man of letters was underwritten by
his occupation as a school inspector. Both Arnold and Mill undoubtedly
looked upon this daily work as important, and Mill's direct contribution
to the formulation of Indian policy certainly was.

3. *Middlemarch:* The Romance of Vocation

1. Quotations are from the Riverside ed. of *Middlemarch,* ed. Gordon
S. Haight (Boston: Houghton Mifflin, 1956).

2. *The Mill on the Floss* (Edinburgh and London: William Black-
wood and Sons, 1861), bk. IV, ch. 3, p. 363.

3. Humphrey House, *The Dickens World,* 2nd ed. (London: Oxford
University Press, 1961), p. 46.

4. Ibid., p. 39.

5. The phrase is George Eliot's in her essay on Rheil, "The Natural History of German Life," included in the edition by Thomas Pinney, *Essays of George Eliot* (New York: Columbia University Press, 1963), p. 25.

6. Acts 9:3-7, 22:6-11, 26:13-18, Galatians 1:13-17.

7. Benjamin Jowett, *Theological Writings* (New York: Henry Frowde, 1902), p. 24; A. D. Nock, *Conversion* (London: Oxford University Press, 1933), esp. chs. 1 and 2; William James, *The Varieties of Religious Experience* (New York: Longmans, Green & Co., 1902), lectures 9 and 10.

8. Georg Lukàcs, *The Historical Novel*, trans. H. and S. Mitchell (first published Moscow, 1937; Boston: Beacon Press, 1962), p. 45.

9. Northrop Frye, *The Anatomy of Criticism* (Princeton: Princeton University Press, 1957), pp. 148, 192-93, 222.

10. Michael Fixler, *Milton and the Kingdoms of God* (Chicago: University of Chicago Press, 1964).

4. *Middlemarch:* Origins and Taxonomy

1. Max Weber, *The Protestant Ethic and the Spirit of Capitalism*, trans. Talcott Parsons (New York: Charles Scribner's Sons, 1958), p. 161.

2. The material in the following paragraphs is based on A. M. Carr-Saunders and P. A. Wildon, *The Professions* (London: Oxford University Press, 1933), and W. J. Reaser, *Professional Men* (New York: Basic Books, 1966).

3. It is interesting to note the proliferation of meanings grouped around "text," "textile," and "tissue," a play made possible by the etymological roots of "text" in the Latin *texere,* to weave. Thus, from one root we find interconnecting references to (1) Lydgate's search for a primary tissue, (2) Mr. Vincy's occupation as a repressive and shoddy silk-manufacturer and the Industrial Revolution in general, (3) the endless web-imagery of the novel, and, of course, (4) the text of the novel itself.

4. "The Intellectual Background of the Novel," in Barbara Hardy, ed., *Critical Approaches to Middlemarch* (London: University of London, The Athelone Press, 1967), pp. 25-38.

5. Charles Joseph Singer, *A History of Biology to about the Year 1900,* 3rd and rev. ed. (London: Aberlard-Schuman, 1959), pp. 103-106.

6. Edward W. Said, "Narrative Quest for Origins and the Discovery of the Mausoleum," *Salmagundi,* no. 12 (Spring 1970), pp. 63-75.

7. In the *Quarry* for *Middlemarch,* one of the alternative outcomes for Will's life when he thinks it is impossible to return to Dorothea is to emigrate to a utopian community "in the West."

8. For the kind of competition a man of science should be able to withstand, see Weber's essay "Science as a Vocation," in *From Max Weber,* ed. and trans. H. H. Garth and C. Wright Mills (New York: Oxford University Press, 1946), p. 134.

9. Lydgate is right to think of medicine as a profession in which a man can rise on the strength of his own talent, for indeed, family connections were of little use in furthering a medical career: one simply did or did not attract patients. The requisite talent, however, was not of the clinical and scientific variety Lydgate has in mind. Since medical knowledge was so paltry, physicians succeeded on the basis of an attractive and authoritative manner, that is, on their ability to make people trust them and believe that they were in complete control (see Reader, *Professional Men,* pp. 30-32).

10. Michel Foucault, *The Order of Things,* no trans. (New York: Pantheon Books, 1970), ch. 5 "Classifying."

11. Farebrother's preoccupation with taxonomy is not an adequate way of looking at the world, either. When he prejudges Lydgate in the Raffles affair, Farebrother demonstrates that correlating superficial similarities and dissimilarities is not the same as penetrating to the deeper history and structure beneath the surfaces of events.

12. See Christopher Hill, *Puritanism and Revolution* (New York: Schocken Books, 1964), ch. 14, "Clarissa Harlowe and Her Times," remarks on romantic love versus property marriage.

5. *Middlemarch:* Indirection and Identification

1. "George Eliot in *Middlemarch,*" in Boris Ford, ed., *From Dickens to Hardy* (Baltimore: Penguin Books, 1958), pp. 274ff.

2. "*Middlemarch* and Science: Problems of Life and Mind," *Review of English Studies,* n.s. 22 (1971): 151ff.

3. The following is based on J. F. C. Harrison, *Quest For the New Moral World: Robert Owen and the Owenites in Britain and America* (New York: Charles Scribner's Sons, 1969).

4. New Harmony *Gazette,* vol. 1 (October 1825), quoted in Harrison, *Quest,* p. 59.

5. The German Jewish thinker Franz Rosenweig, in discussing the commandment to love one's neighbor as one's self, catches this notion of the neighbor as "the *nearest* neighbor precisely at the moment of love, the one who is nighest to me, at least at this moment, regardless of what he may have been before or will be afterward. He is not loved for his own sake . . . another could easily stand in his place precisely at this place nearest me" (*The Star of Redemption,* trans. W. H. Hallo [New York: Holt, Rinehart and Winston, 1970], p. 218).

6. U. C. Knoepflmacher, *Religious Humanism and the Novel* (Princeton: Princeton University Press, 1965), p. 101. Remarriage is, interestingly, a violation of the Comtian dogma of "perpetual widowhood." Compare this with the marriage (a de facto second marriage) of Marian Evans-George Eliot and the responses to it in Gordon S. Haight, *George Eliot: A Biography* (New York: Oxford University Press, 1968), pp. 338-339.

7. Note that Dorothea's development can be read as progress away from a self-dramatizing sainthood on the Puritan model at the opening of the novel and toward a more authentic "humanistic" sainthood here. For Dorothea's choice of Will as an act contributing to her elevation as a saint, see Robert F. Damm, "Sainthood and Dorothea Brooke," *The Victorian Newsletter* (Spring 1969), pp. 18-22. Dorothea's change might also be interpreted as a transition from an activist conception of sainthood, in the spirit of Saint Theresa, to a more conventional quietist role.

8. W. J. Harvey, "The Intellectual Background of the Novel" in Barbara Hardy, ed., *Critical Approaches to Middlemarch* (London: University of London, the Athelone Press, 1967), pp. 25-38.

9. Aviva Gottlieb, "George Eliot's 'Casaubon tints,' " *Scripta Hierosolymitana* (Jerusalem), vol. 25 (1973).

10. Gordon S. Haight, ed., *The George Eliot Letters* (New Haven: Yale University Press, 1954-   ), V:29 (8 May 1868); V:229 (28 December 1871); V:301 (19 August 1872); V:160 (7 July 1871).

6. *Middlemarch:* Choice and Evasion

1. For a more systematic classification of the ways of making a living from politics, including that of the journalist, see Weber, "Politics as a Vocation," in *From Max Weber*, ed. and trans. H. H. Garth and C. Wright Mills (New York: Oxford University Press, 1946) pp. 77-129.

2. See Michael Birks, *Gentleman of the Law* (London: Stevens, 1960), and Brian Abel-Smith, *Lawyers and the Courts: A Sociological Study of the English Legal System, 1750-1965* (Cambridge, Mass.: Harvard University Press, 1967).

3. Ironically, extending some sort of patronage to Will is discussed elsewhere in the novel. Sir James and Mrs. Cadwaller, aghast at the idea that Will should ever be thought a suitor of Dorothea's, suggest that Casaubon find some way to get him shipped abroad as an ambassdor's attaché.

4. "Original" in its adjectival meaning of an inventive person who does things not known to have been done before is a distinctly nineteenth-century coinage, according to the *OED*. An example given there from Jowett (Plato, 2nd ed., 1875) sounds as if it had jumped out of the pages

of *Middlemarch:* "A great original genius struggling with unequal conditions of knowledge."

5. Jerome Beaty, "History by Indirection: The Era of Reform in *Middlemarch," Victorian Studies,* 1 (December 1957): 173-179.

6. The opening of chapter 19 is an example of this double notation: "When George the Fourth was still reigning over the privacies of Windsor, when the Duke of Wellington was Prime Minister, and Mr. Vincy was mayor of the old corporation of Middlemarch, Mrs. Casaubon, born Dorothea Brooke, had taken her wedding journey to Rome." See also the opening of chapter 46.

7. The phrase is Michael York Mason's from an admirable article, *"Middlemarch* and History," *Nineteenth-Century Fiction,* 25 (1971): 417-431.

8. For the changing nature of this job, see F. M. L. Thompson, *English Landed Society in the Nineteenth Century* (London: Routledge & K. Paul, 1963), pp. 68, 322.

9. J. F. C. Harrison, *Quest for the New Moral World: Robet Owen and the Owenites in Britain and America* (New York: Charles Scribner's Sons, 1969), pp. 202-207.

10. Shlomo Avineri, *The Social and Political Thought of Karl Marx* (London: Cambridge University Press, 1968), p. 104.

11. Ibid.

12. W. J. Reader, *Professional Men* (New York: Basic Books, 1966), p. 59.

13. "The clergy in England, it is clear, was not a priesthood but a rational occupation for a gentleman" (Reader, *Professional Men,* p. 13).

14. I am grateful to Alan Silver for suggesting this comparison.

15. Note that *Middlemarch* is alone in this connection among the later novels. The plots of *Felix Holt* (the histories of Esther Lyon and Harold Transome) and *Daniel Deronda* (the story of Deronda's concealed Jewishness) rely, at least formally, on the device of hidden paternity.

16. Weber, *Protestant Ethic,* pp. 122, 137.

7. *Daniel Deronda* and the Messianic Calling

1. *Daniel Deronda,* ed. Barbara Hardy (Baltimore: Penguin, 1967).

2. This passage from *Middlemarch* makes an interesting comparison with the closing paragraph of Dickens' *Little Dorrit* (1865-1867) in which the domestic calm surrounding Arthur Clennam and Little Dorrit as they leave church on their wedding day is contrasted with the "roaring streets" of London: "And as they passed along in sunshine and shade, the noisy and the eager, and the arrogant and the forward and the vain, fretted and chafed, and made their usual uproar."

3. George Eliot's phrase "local habitation" quoted in the preceding paragraph is from *A Midsummer Night's Dream*, V.i.17. Theseus is speaking about similarities among lovers, madmen, and poets: "And as imagination bodies forth/The forms of things unknown, the poet's pen/Turns them to shapes, and gives to airy nothing/A local habitation and a name." The continuation of the line "and a name" includes what Deronda acquires when his Jewish ancestry is revealed to him. The original context of the quotation is concerned with George Eliot, who here takes pride in her ability to conjure up Deronda and envision an as-yet existing habitation for him. We, however, are not so convinced.

8. Epilogue: The Craft of Society and the Vocation of Art

1. *New Grub Street* (Boston: Houghton Mifflin Company, 1962). See Edward Said, *Beginnings: Method and Intention* (New York: Basic Books, 1975), pp. 139ff.

2. *The Autobiography of Mark Rutherford, Dissenting Minister,* "ed. by his friend Reuben Shapcott" (New York: G. P. Putnam's Sons, 1881).

3. For Rutherford, as for Mill sixty years earlier, reading Wordsworth is the beginning of reintegration and reaffirmation. Although it is not clear which Wordsworth Rutherford read—*The Prelude* had been published in his time but not in Mill's—the poetry obviously served not only as a legitimation of the affective dimension of life but also as assurance that beyond the world of both theology and positivism there was a coherent and mysterious order of nature to which man, in the absence of other norms, could trust himself. Wordsworth represents the most important stage in the secularization of the Miltonic legacy concerning the poetic vocation.

4. *Robert Elsmere* by Mrs. Humphry Ward (London: Smith, Elder & Co., 1905), first published 1888.

5. *My Apprenticeship* (London: Longmans, Green & Co., 1926), p. 133.

6. Much later, in the 1930s, humanity was to be rehabilitated as an object of worship in the form of the Soviet state. In their effusion upon their return from Russia, the Webbs testified that they had seen the realization of Utopia.

7. *Portrait of the Artist as a Young Man,* the corrected Dublin holograph (New York: Viking Press, 1964).

INDEX